Literature Circles
in
Middle School:
One Teacher's Journey

Literature Circles
in
Middle School:
One Teacher's Journey

by

Bonnie Campbell Hill

Katherine L. Schlick Noe

and Janine A. King

Christopher-Gordon Publishers, Inc.
Norwood, Massachusetts

Copyright Acknowledgments

Every effort has been made to contact copyright holders for permission to reproduce borrowed material where necessary. We apologize for any oversights and would be happy to rectify them in future printings.

All student work used with permission.

Copyright © 2003 by Christopher-Gordon Publishers, Inc.

All rights reserved. Except for review purposes, no part of this material protected by this copyright notice may be reproduced or utilized in any form or by any means, electronic or mechanical, including photocopying, recording, or in any information and retrieval system, without the express written permission of the publisher or copyright holder.

Christopher-Gordon Publishers, Inc.

1502 Providence Highway, Suite #12
Norwood, Massachusetts 02062

800-934-8322
781-762-5577

Printed in the United State of America
10 9 8 7 6 5 4 3 2 1   07 06 05 04 03 02

ISBN: 1-929024-50-9
Library of Congress Catalogue Number: 2002112038

Acknowledgments

We are grateful to the students in Janine's middle school classrooms whose openness, insights, and energy created this story. We are also indebted to the colleagues, family members, and reviewers who read this manuscript. Their thoughtful feedback and suggestions helped us solve many of our writing challenges: Janet Allen, Laura Benson, Carrie Ekey, Cindy Flegenheimer, Nancy Florig, Laura Hill, Nancy J. Johnson, Anne Klein, Christian Knoeller, Ken Lundberg, Linda Rief, Cynthia Ruptic, Myra Vinson, and Carol Wilcox. Sue Canavan and Hiram Howard support every project we bring them, and for this we are very thankful. As always, our gratitude goes to Steve Hill for his endurance in formatting the illustrations and figures and for his creativity in designing the database and CD-ROM. Finally, we deeply appreciate the faith and support of our families.

Contents

Table of Figures

Introduction

Last September, Bonnie Campbell Hill and Katherine Schlick Noe persuaded Janine King that writing a book together about literature circles in her middle school classroom would be a simple project. And

Authors, from left to right: Bonnie Campbell Hill, Katherine L. Schlick Noe, and Janine A. King.

she fell for it. We began by "picking her brain" as we met each month, and Janine articulated how literature circles worked with middle school students and how they had changed over time. Bonnie and Katherine took notes and Janine collected student samples. We crafted drafts, sent multiple e-mails back and forth, and the book slowly took shape.

Over the years, the three of us have collaborated on numerous professional presentations, and Bonnie and Katherine have co-authored three other books on literature circles. Yet, in this book, you'll hear just one voice—Janine's. We wanted you to feel as if you're walking into her classroom, listening in on her deliberations, and making teaching decisions alongside her. We had to find a way to accomplish this without overwhelming the book with voices or writing in the distant third person. So the three of us wrote in the first person, contributing equally to telling the story that unfolds.

The Structure of This Book

When we read professional books, we don't want generalities. We crave details and examples in order to picture how the ideas might really work in a classroom. Therefore, we have included quotes and writing from Janine's students, and she has been honest about her successes and failures. We have also tried to capture how literature circles have changed in Janine's classroom over the past few years.

In middle school, early adolescents are simultaneously honing their reading and writing skills and trying to figure out their place in the larger world. Chapter 1 sets a context for literature circles with this unique and energetic age group. We explain where literature circles fit in Janine's middle school language arts curriculum and how they meet some of the unique needs of young adolescents. In chapters 2 and 3 we provide specific examples of how Janine plans her literature circle units each year. We also talk about how she selects books, including lists of some of the titles and literature circle units she has found successful at various grade levels.

Conversation is at the core of literature circles. We describe how Janine helps students learn to talk about books independently in chapter 4. We explain how she supports students' responses through writing in chapter 5 and how she has changed the expectations and format each year as she seeks to elicit quality work from her students. Chapter 6 addresses extending students' response to literature through the arts. We have included lists of possible extension projects, as well as ways that these responses can help students to dig deeper into the books they are reading. In chapters 4 through 6, we include specific focus lessons that Janine has used and examples of how she evaluates students. We conclude each chapter with some last thoughts about Janine's next steps in her journey as a learner, a teacher, a reader, and a writer.

Database of Young Adult Books

The database for *Literature Circles in Middle School: One Teacher's Journey* contains over 750 young adult book titles. You can add your own comments to the existing entries or add your own titles. The database is in both PC and Mac formats. Instructions for installing and using the database are found on pages 145 and 146.

Chapter 1

Literature Circles in My
Middle School Classroom

I feel like I am part of the story. I am there, I am participating in all of the events, but I can't change what happens. I'm along for the ride. It makes me feel like the author is writing the book for me.

—Alex, Grade 6

It is 8:40 a.m. on a Monday. School officially starts in five minutes, but Hillary is already there, waiting to talk to me. "I know that I am reading *Elizabeth I* [Lasky, 1999] for literature circles, but I wondered if I could borrow a copy of *Mary, Bloody Mary* [Meyer, 1999] to read on my own." Tuesday morning, she is back again, this time with a warning: "When you read this book, be sure you don't have anything else important to do. I read the whole book last night! I couldn't put it down. Do you have any more books that are this good?"

Over the next few days, Hillary read *Beware, Princess Elizabeth* (Meyer, 2001), *The Shakespeare Stealer* (Blackwood, 1998), *Shakespeare's Scribe* (Blackwood, 2000), and *King of Shadows* (Cooper, 1999) and clamored for more books about the same time period. This is every middle school teacher's dream—to ignite a student's passion for reading. Hillary's experience embodies the power of literature circles—a synergy of good books, an engaging topic, and the opportunity to collaborate through reading, writing, and discussion.

Why Literature Circles?

I was always excited about teaching language arts in middle school because I love to read. I had great visions of my students loving it as much as I do. However, I found out right away that there can be a difference between loving to read and loving to teach reading. With the teacher's manual open on my desk, I had a hard time choosing what was valuable and what wasn't. All of those questions and activities overwhelmed me. We could spend 3 weeks on just one story. My students looked at me like the torture was deliberate. I had to find a new way to teach reading.

Even though I love to read, I can't just say, "OK, we're going to sit and read," and call that a reading program. Being in an adult book group helped me to think about how I wanted to teach. My favorite part of my book club was discovering new things about the books that I hadn't thought of on my own. I knew I wanted that for my students.

So I began to put the pieces together. I started reading aloud, and my students enjoyed that. Then we started writing about our reading and we started to talk. That's how I fell into literature circles. I wanted to find a way to structure my language arts program around reading, thinking, talking, writing, and extending response through the arts. I realize now that I was laying the groundwork for literature circles even before I knew anything about them.

What Are Literature Circles?

In literature circles, small groups of students read the same book and collectively construct meaning as they respond through discussions, writing, and the arts. In my middle school classes, literature circles function much like my adult book group—but without the food and wine. The purpose is simultaneously simple and complex: to read and explore books, characters, issues, and ideas and to figure out what we think on our own and with other people. I like JoAnn

Portalupi's (Fletcher & Portalupi, 2001, p. 74) description of literature circles as "lingering in a text." Through reading, talking, writing, and responding in a variety of ways, students gain a better sense of what they think, what they value, and what they can do with what they know.

Although several professional resources describe the structure and refinement of literature circles at the elementary school level (e.g., Daniels, 2002; Hill, Johnson, & Schlick Noe, 1995; Samway & Whang, 1995; Schlick Noe & Johnson, 1999), this book focuses specifically on literature circles in middle school.

How Can Literature Circles Meet the Needs of Middle School Students?

Looking back at my frustrations those first years, I realize that many teachers have shared those same feelings. My teaching didn't match what my students needed, as learners or as adolescents. Literature circles have helped me to align my teaching with my students' needs and interests.

Figure 1-1 summarizes some of the needs that adolescent students carry with them into the middle school classroom (Combs, 1997) and suggests ways that our teaching can help.

If you ask students what they like best about literature circles, they often say that they like choosing the book they want to read, picking the topics and questions to discuss, and deciding what type of extension project best fits the book. As adolescents, they appreciate choice as a way of demonstrating their growing competence and independence in the world. In their book, *"Reading Don't Fix No Chevys": Literacy in the Lives of Young Men* (Smith & Wilhelm, 2002), the authors state, "By far the most prevalent piece of advice our boys offered to teachers was to give students choices" (p. 197).

As a language arts teacher, I use my time efficiently and meaningfully. I would rather read books and mark teaching points with Post-it® notes than create short-answer questions about every novel. Instead of correcting quizzes, I can spend my time listening in on discussions, taking anecdotal notes, and writing quick responses in students' journals. This provides authentic assessment information for me and valuable

Needs	Meeting Needs
• Some control over their learning materials	• Choice in reading materials and writing topics
• Understanding a purpose for what they are doing	• Reading and writing for real purposes
• Connections	• Reading and writing integrated across subjects • Reading and writing about characters and topics they can relate to • Connections with others who will listen, read, and respond respectfully to their ideas
• Opportunities to make decisions	• Students involved in own learning and evaluation
• Time for social interaction	• Discussion and collaboration with peers as a constant part of learning
• Adult relationships away from home	• Teachers interact with students through conferences, interviews, and sharing own reading and writing

Figure 1-1: Needs of Adolescents

feedback for my students. I also find that students write and talk about issues and questions I might never have thought to raise. Literature circles have enriched our collective lives as readers and writers.

What Is the Role of Literature Circles in My Middle School Language Arts Program?

In grades 6, 7, and 8, my students continue their long journey as learners. I've organized my language arts program to guide students' literacy growth throughout the year. We analyze and craft poetry. We write persuasive, expository, narrative, and procedural pieces. Students make oral presentations. We examine the technical intricacies of grammar, spelling, and punctuation. In short, we work hard to develop all of the attitudes and abilities of literate people.

However, if we stopped there, I wouldn't be doing my job. Why would students go to all the trouble to learn how to read, write, speak, and listen well if they never get to *use* those skills as real readers and writers? What good are literacy skills if you *choose* not to use them? Literature circles are by no means my entire language arts curriculum, but they're a big part of it. They provide a key component: the enticing opportunity to practice and refine literacy strategies through interactions with peers and high-quality books.

Literature circles help me to meet three essential responsibilities as a middle school teacher: to align my instruction with state standards, to assess my students authentically, and to guide students to become engaged, independent, and confident learners.

Meeting State Standards

Like most states, Washington has developed literacy standards for students at all levels. Literature circles represent good instruction to help students meet these standards. In Appendix A, I show how many of my focus lessons in literature circles address the Washington state standards for listening, speaking, reading, and writing. For example, through students' discussions, writing, and extension projects, I know how well they understand what they've read. As they read aloud to back up their opinions, I can check for fluency. Writing about literature fosters students' facility with different forms of writing. Literature circles naturally integrate a broad range of literacy skills and strategies.

Assessing Students Authentically

Literature circles can provide a more authentic method of measuring students' skills as readers and writers than a multiple-choice or short-answer test. It sometimes feels a bit risky when you don't have an answer key. You have to trust that you will recognize what students have learned through what they say, write, and create. This can seem intimidating. However, the first time I listened to an in-depth discussion, I was amazed at their thinking. Looking over my anecdotal notes, I realized that I had more insight into students' comprehension and vocabulary sophistication from a single discussion than I had gathered previously from a test over an entire unit.

Guiding Students as Learners

All year long I share strategies that good readers use, such as jotting down questions during reading, finding evidence in the text, reading like a writer, savoring new words, and questioning the text. We then apply those strategies during literature circles. We collect quotes from the book and use Post-it® notes to mark passages. Students come to understand how using evidence can clarify a point and strengthen an opinion.

In addition, students learn to be active participants in their own learning through literature circles. In many ways, grading a test would be easier, but when I choose the questions, I'm telling my students how to think about the book. When students take the lead, they have to be thoughtful. Students take an active role when you challenge them: "You come up with the questions. You tell *me,* what is it about this book that's good?" They begin to realize that there is more than one right answer. That's why I love blank pieces of paper and open-ended conversations.

Literature circles also help students to understand literary elements in a meaningful way. Former students tell me that this emphasis provides a good foundation for success in high school. Recently, Crissa, a high school sophomore, dropped by. "I just took midterms and felt totally prepared. We were tested on the same types of things we did in eighth grade in literature circles," she said. "It really helped to know how to write about the plot and tension and conflict in a story, and how to back up my opinion with quotes from the book."

Finally, I think that literature circles are perfect for teaching independence. For example, I don't collect journals every time I give an assignment. Students are responsible for keeping up with their reading and journal entries. They learn that I'm not going to collect the journals for 2 or 3 weeks. To some, this seems an eternity. However, they soon realize that they can't fill an entire journal the night before it's due. They can't fake it. When students don't complete their journals, I tell them, "I don't give tests, but this serves the same purpose. It shows me what you know about the book. When you don't put effort into your entries, it's the same as if you hadn't answered half the questions on a test."

Ultimately, literature circles hook kids into reading. The read-alouds, independent reading, the shared journal entries, and the discussions all become part of the fabric of our classroom. Literature circle conversations allow students to see others in a new light, sometimes breaking down peer group barriers. As we build our skills in literature circles, we weave a community of readers and writers.

The Grading Challenge

In the end—after the reading, talking, writing, and extending—comes the grading. In my middle school, grading is the outcome of all of the assessments I've gathered as I listen, observe, and read student work. One of the most frequent concerns that teachers raise about using literature circles in middle school is grading. Finding ways to provide authentic, accurate, and growth-inducing evaluation, and then to translate that into letter grades is a challenge that I must meet.

I have divided the language arts grade for reading into five components (Figure 1-2): discussion, response journals, extension projects, independent reading, and content area reading. The first three components are evaluated through literature circles and share equal weight because we spend approximately the same amount of time on each. Independent reading is evaluated separately, based on reading logs, Friday Book Talks (explained more fully in chapter 2), and my observations of students choosing books and reading on their own. The grade for content area reading is based on skills and strategies built during instruction that takes place between lit-

Literature Discussions	25%
Response Journals	25%
Extension Projects	25%
Independent Reading	15%
Content Area Reading	10%
TOTAL	100%

Figure 1-2: Reading Grades

erature circle units. This constitutes a smaller portion of the grade because it is reinforced and covered more extensively in students' social studies, science, and mathematics classes.

I use a 4-point scale to determine the grade for each of these five aspects of reading:

> 4 = Exceeds standards
>
> 3 = Meets standards
>
> 2 = Approaches standards
>
> 1 = Below standards

Specifics about grading will be addressed in chapter 4 (Discussions), chapter 5 (Written Response), and chapter 6 (Extension Projects).

Successful Literature Circles in Middle School

When I first started teaching, I was constantly on the lookout for just the right programs, teaching methods, and tricks that would make instruction more meaningful and hopefully a little easier in my classroom. With every workshop I attended and every professional book I read, I hoped to find a formula to follow word for word. However, when I tried to follow another educator's ideas down to the minute-by-minute plan so that I would experience the same success, I was always disappointed. Finally, I realized that I had to take in the ideas, methods, and concepts, then use what worked for me, make it my own, and discard the rest. We all have different schedules, students, and personalities. When we try to imitate exactly what another teacher does, it doesn't fit.

In this book, you will find the way I do literature circles in my middle school classroom and the adjustments I have made to match my situation and needs as they have changed. This is what works for me. As you read this book, we hope that you will pull out some of the ideas, give them a try, add in your own successful methods, then mold them into what works for you. We have purposely chosen not to include a step-by-step schedule of what I do every day, every week, and every month. Instead, we have tried to capture the big picture of what literature circles in my classroom look like and some background information showing my evolution over time.

My expertise and confidence with literature circles have grown gradually. I rely on my professional colleagues for ideas and problem solving. I also find inspiration in other professional books about reading and writing in middle school. The professional books listed in Figure 1-3 have been particularly helpful for planning my middle school language arts program.

It all comes down to this: You have to have confidence in this way of teaching and faith in your students. You also need to trust yourself as a teacher and a reader. Using literature circles has made me even more of a reader, which makes me more interested in helping my students become readers. I am able to give my students room to be themselves. From day to day and year to year, my students continue to amaze me with their innocence, their sophistication, their passion, their boredom, their intensity, their emotions, their wisdom, and their grace. I feel very privileged each year to watch them blossom as readers and writers. I hope that your journey is equally enjoyable.

Book Club for Middle School by Taffy E. Raphael, Marcella Kehus, and Karen Damphousse

Developing Competent Readers in the Middle Grades by Martha Combs

Getting Started With Literature Circles by Katherine L. Schlick Noe and Nancy J. Johnson

I Read It, but I Don't Get It: Comprehension Strategies for Adolescent Readers by Cris Tovani

In the Middle: New Understandings About Writing, Reading, and Learning by Nancie Atwell

Literature Circles and Response by Bonnie Campbell Hill, Nancy J. Johnson, and Katherine L. Schlick Noe

The Literature Circles Resource Guide by Bonnie Campbell Hill, Katherine L. Schlick Noe, and Nancy J. Johnson

Literature Circles: Voice and Choice in Book Clubs and Reading Groups by Harvey Daniels

Literature Study Circles in a Multicultural Classroom by Katharine Davies Samway and Gail Whang

Practical Approaches for Teaching Reading and Writing in Middle Schools by Teresa Morretta and Michelle Ambrosini

"Reading Don't Fix No Chevys": Literacy in the Lives of Young Men by Michael W. Smith and Jeffrey D. Wilhelm

Seeking Diversity: Language Arts With Adolescents by Linda Rief

Strategies that Work: Teaching Comprehension to Enhance Understanding by Stephanie Harvey and Anne Goudvis

Struggling Adolescent Readers: A Collection of Teaching Strategies, edited by David W. Moore, Donna E. Alvermann, and Kathleen A. Hinchman

Teaching Reading in Middle School: A Strategic Approach to Teaching Reading That Improves Comprehension and Thinking by Laura Robb

There's Room for Me Here: Literacy Workshop in the Middle School by Janet Allen and Kyle Gonzalez

To Be a Boy, To Be a Reader: Engaging Teen and Preteen Boys in Active Literacy by William G. Brozo

Vision and Voice: Extending the Literacy Spectrum by Linda Rief

What Adolescents Deserve: A Commitment to Students' Literacy Learning, edited by James A. Rycik and Judith Irwin

Yellow Brick Roads: Shared and Guided Paths to Independent Reading 4–12 by Janet Allen

You Gotta BE the Book: Teaching Engaged and Reflective Reading with Adolescents by Jeffrey D. Wilhelm

Figure 1-3: Professional Books on Middle School Literacy

Chapter 2

Organizing Literature Circles

Being able to choose a book is like when you go out to a restaurant, you choose what you want to eat and what sounds good to you, instead of going to Aunt Freta's house and having to eat pickled beets!

—Tony, Grade 8

I walk a very fine line with literature circles. My middle school students crave choice, flexibility, and autonomy. They are full of emotions and energy. They hate restrictions. I have to figure out how to let them own their response to books and discussions, but not abdicate my responsibility as coach and guide. Organizing effective literature circles in middle school takes the instincts of a lion tamer, the skill of an engineer, and the finesse of a diplomat. I've tried to develop a format that promotes choice, independence, and individual responsibility, while also providing an effective and predictable structure.

This chapter describes my organizational framework for literature circles in sixth, seventh, and eighth grades. I'll describe how I lay a foundation for response even before the first groups meet. Then I'll walk you through my year, explaining how I launch literature circles and help students to internalize the various components. In chapters 3 through 6, I go into more detail about the specifics of selecting books, supporting quality discussion and written response, and guiding students to extend response through the arts.

Getting Started

Some of my colleagues in the elementary grades wait until October or November to start literature circles because they want to spend time developing expectations and building a sense of community. However, in middle school, I jump into literature circles the first week of school. I want my students to start reading and writing the first day and to know that this is what we will do all year.

Whole-Class Novel

As we lay the foundation for literature circles, I've found that it works best to have the whole class read the same novel. This sets the stage, providing guided practice with all components of literature circles that students will later apply more independently in their groups formed around book choices. Beginning the year with all students reading the same book gives them a chance to develop the skills, strategies, and behaviors that create the foundation for successful literature circles throughout the year. For this first unit, I choose an engaging book that is accessible to all of my students. This is often a short novel that will lead into a longer book. For example, the sixth graders read *Song of the Trees* (1975) then follow up with *Roll of Thunder, Hear My Cry* (1976), both by Mildred Taylor. This first unit is a training session, so it's important to go slowly, provide clear modeling, and review my expectations often.

Forming Literature Circle Groups

I find that groups of four or five students work the best. Larger groups tend to break off into smaller conversations, and groups with only three students don't seem to have enough energy or diversity of ideas. I form these first groups myself, making them as heterogeneous as possible by balancing personalities, gender, and ability levels.

Later, when students choose from an array of books, I form the groups according to students' choices. I "booktalk" each of the novels, describe some enticing aspects of the book, and give students an idea of the number of pages and level of difficulty. At this point, many students are just looking at the cover and thinking about the length of the book. I want them to go inside the book, so I take advantage of this opportunity to reinforce strategies for selecting an appropriate and enticing book. I explain the different characteristics that determine interest and accessibility, such as dialect, vocabulary, format, length, and text organization. The best way to teach this is to show examples of each characteristic. For instance, I point out how Chris Crutcher used letters from Beau Brewster to Larry King as a stylistic device in *Ironman* (1995) and read aloud a couple of powerful passages. I also reinforce familiarity with book features by pointing them out in the books I'm reading aloud.

After they've heard about each book, students take time to examine copies of all of the choices. I suggest that they read a page or two to get a sense of the characters and the overall flavor of the book. Students vote for a first, second, and third choice on a ballot. In my class, this ballot is a blank piece of recycled paper; other teachers use preprinted forms. I can form groups in just a few minutes, honoring each student's first choice whenever possible. However, I also make some strategic decisions about which students work well together (or not!) and ensure that there are both outgoing and more reticent students balanced among the groups. Another deliberate step I take is to provide books on tape or other forms of assistance for students who need additional support. (More about meeting the needs of diverse learners is included in chapter 3.)

I've found that this whole process lessens the chance that students will choose books that don't appeal to them or are inappropriate for their reading level. Most important, I'm placing the responsibility for choosing books where it belongs—in students' hands.

Brainstorming to Launch Discussions

I know that those first discussions are going to be ragged, but we have to start somewhere. Students gradually construct their understanding of literature circle conversations through experience and guidance. After students have read several chapters of the whole-class novel, we prepare for discussion with a short brainstorming session. I ask the class, "What are some things in these first chapters that you could talk about fruitfully in your groups?" I record their ideas on the board for students to refer to during the discussion.

For example, the seventh graders suggested the following topics about *Jason's Gold* (Hobbs, 1999):

- Jason's challenges
- Time period (What was it like?)
- What you would do if you were Jason
- The characters' traits and interactions

At this point students ran out of ideas, so I stepped in and offered several more:

- Setting (location)
- Predictions
- Events that might affect the ending
- Author's style

As you can see, I try to strike a balance between allowing students freedom to choose their own topics and guiding their discussion. How much guidance I provide depends on the groups and my goals for a particular literature circle unit. In the *Jason's Gold* unit, for example, I knew that students needed a clear sense of place and the historical time frame for the novel in order to understand what happens to the characters. For that reason, I made sure their discussions included some key literary elements and historical information.

Determining a Weekly Schedule

On Mondays we set up a reading schedule. I tell students how many weeks they have to read the book. During the first unit, we plan the weekly reading schedule together. I show students how to divide the number of pages in the book by the number of reading days available. Modeling this process early on prepares students to create their own reading schedules in later units when they will choose from a variety of books. We don't count on weekends. Instead, students can use the weekend if they need a little extra time to catch up.

Each student records the schedule on a bookmark. On the back of the bookmark, students record interesting words from the book and questions to bring to the discussion. Figure 2-1 shows Laura's bookmark from *Mary, Bloody Mary* (Meyer, 1999).

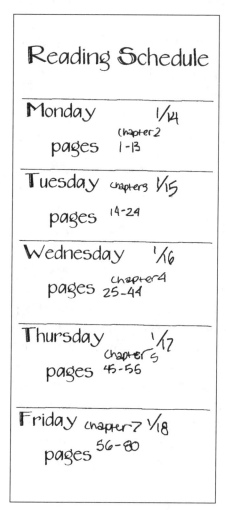
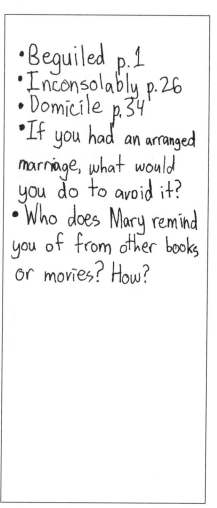

Figure 2-1: Reading Bookmark

Every Monday, we update the week's schedule on a new bookmark with the targeted completion date in mind. Because students read during class, we may need to adjust the schedule for intrusions such as snow days, field trips, and assemblies. At this point, group members check in with each other to see if the number of pages they have scheduled to read each day works for everyone. If it was too overwhelming, or if they are hooked and eager to finish the book, the students adjust their reading schedule accordingly. Making collaborative decisions about the number of pages to read is one of the focus lessons I teach early in the process. This not only helps students develop time management skills but also builds skills for consensus and allows students to take responsibility for decision making.

To fuel a good discussion, students need to be far enough into a book to care about the characters but not so far that they can't remember details. Each group usually meets for a discussion once a week, resulting in three discussions during the course of reading the book: one near the beginning, one in the middle, and a final discussion after students have completed the whole novel.

I've found that breaking the book into three sections for discussions works well. In the first third of a novel, students get to know the characters and their problems and issues. This first part of a book lends itself to conversations about what might happen, characters' motives for their actions, and where the story is headed. Near the middle of a book, I often overhear discussions about why characters might react in a certain way or about the underlying issues and problems they are confronting. This is when I hear readers talk about the author's style and make connections to their own lives and other books. When they finish the book, students talk about how their predictions came true or not, how they might have responded in similar situations, and what they liked or disliked about the book. Students are also required to write two journal entries each week (chapter 5). At the end of the unit, they create an extension project based on the book (chapter 6). When students are not discussing, they are expected to use class time to read or to write in their journals.

Weekly Schedule: Daily Classes

When I first started using literature circles in my classroom, I saw my students every day for a 45-minute period just for reading. Figure 2-2 shows my schedule for a typical literature circle week.

Monday	5–15 min. 10–30 min.	Set reading schedule for the week. Discuss journal topics. Students begin to read and write in journals.
Tuesday	10–20 min. 10–30 min.	Focus lessons (see chapters 4, 5, and 6) Two or three groups discuss. Other students read or write in journals.
Wednesday	10–20 min. 10–30 min.	Focus lessons (see chapters 4, 5, and 6) Two or three groups discuss. Other students read or write in journals.
Thursday	45 min.	Students read or write in journals.
Friday	45 min.	Independent reading day (self-selected books)

Figure 2-2: Typical Weekly Schedule (Daily Classes)

Monday sets the stage for the week. We planned the reading and discussion schedule and discussed potential journal topics. Any time left over was devoted to reading literature circle books and writing responses. Discussions took place on Tuesday and Wednesday. With only a few groups meeting each day, I was able to listen in on the discussions and take anecdotal notes. The whole class continued reading their literature circle books and writing in their journals on Thursday, while I circulated through the room to check on students' progress. Throughout the year, Fridays were reserved for independent reading of self-selected books.

Weekly Schedule: Block Classes

I currently teach at a middle school that has implemented a block schedule. I meet with students three times a week on Monday and Wednesday or Tuesday and Thursday for 90 minutes and on Friday for 45 minutes. I devote approximately half of the language arts period to reading (45 minutes) and half to writing (45 minutes). In Figure 2-3 you can see my current block schedule for a typical literature circle week.

Monday or Tuesday	5–15 min. 10–20 min. 10–30 min.	Set reading schedule for the week. Focus lessons Discuss journal writing topics.
	45 min.	Writing instruction
Wednesday or Thursday	10–20 min. 10–30 min. 10–20 min.	Focus lessons All literature groups discuss and debrief. Students read or write in journals.
	45 min.	Writing instruction
Friday	45 min.	Independent reading day (self-selected books)

Figure 2-3: Typical Weekly Schedule (Block Schedule)

Because I see students only 3 days a week, one day (Monday or Tuesday) is devoted to focus lessons and response journals, one day (Wednesday or Thursday) is devoted to discussions, and Friday is used for independent reading. This means that all of the literature circle groups meet to discuss at the same time. I start that day with a quick focus lesson, then listen to groups and take anecdotal notes. We conclude the reading period with a debriefing session. Writing instruction occurs in the second 45 minutes of the language arts block.

Because I teach both reading and writing, I much prefer this type of schedule. It provides longer blocks of time for students to get involved in their learning each day. We spend more time reading and writing and less time moving around. It also allows me to use the time flexibly. For instance, if discussions are going well or students are involved in the extension projects, I may extend the time for reading and allot more time to writing the next week.

As you can see in the schedule, every Friday is devoted to independent reading. I'd like to take a moment to explain how this component of my language arts program reinforces what we do in literature circles. The number one goal I have for my students is that they will become lifelong readers. My hope is that long after reading is required in school, students will still choose to read on their own. As with any other skill, most students need to learn how to become independent readers.

In her book *Seeking Diversity* (1992), Linda Rief makes the powerful point that if we want our students to become readers and writers, we need to give them time to read and write. We also need to model what good readers do. This book inspired me to set Friday aside just for independent reading. We use these 45 minutes each week to share books through book talks and to read the books *we* choose to read. The focus is on books students have chosen for themselves, not those I have assigned. In this way, I hope to support the notion of the independent reader as a member of a community of readers who share and recommend books they love.

Completing a literature circle unit usually takes 3 to 4 weeks for reading, discussions, and written response. I find that many students naturally gravitate toward various art forms to respond to a book. Therefore, we generally culminate the unit with an extension project, described more fully in chapter 6. I usually allow 1 week for students to complete their extension projects during class time.

Determining a Yearly Plan for Literature Circles

I usually plan 4 or 5 literature circle units during the school year. I try to incorporate different genres, such as realistic fiction, adventure, historical fiction, and nonfiction. The books in each unit represent a range of difficulty. Chapter 3 provides more specific information about how I choose books to meet my students' needs. Between literature circle units, I focus on a particular genre, form of writing, or some other area of language arts for 2 to 4 weeks. I find that changing the format for a few weeks keeps students engaged and interested.

At workshops or conferences, teachers often ask me for titles of books I use with my students. This wish for specificity is one of the reasons we wrote this book. Rather than pre-

Books	Skills and Strategies
Unit: Injustice (whole-class books)	

Roll of Thunder, Hear My Cry and *Song of the Trees* by Mildred Taylor	• Literature circle structure
	  Discussions
	  Journals
	• Setting
	• Memorable language

Unit: Ancient Egypt (choice of books)	
Nonfiction books on ancient Egypt	• Reading nonfiction • Text elements: charts, graphs, glossary
Unit: Author Biographies (choice of books)	

Knots in My Yo-Yo String by Jerry Spinelli
My Life in Dog Years by Gary Paulsen
Homesick: My Own Story by Jean Fritz
Boy by Roald Dahl
	• Writing
	  Where authors get ideas
	  Style
	  Voice

Unit: Finding a Place to Belong—Homeless Children (choice of books)	
Randall's Wall by Carole Fenner *Family Pose* by Dean Hughes *Maniac Magee* by Jerry Spinelli *A Place to Call Home* by Jackie French Koller *When the Road Ends* by Jean Thesman	• Understanding theme • Fact vs. opinion • Stereotypes • Character
Unit: Swallowed by Injustice: Japanese-American Internment (choice of books)	
Journey to Topaz by Yoshiko Uchida *Journey Home* by Yoshiko Uchida *The Invisible Thread* by Yoshiko Uchida *The Eternal Spring of Mr. Ito* by Sheila Garrigue	• Understanding theme • Point of view • Author's craft • Compare and Contrast

Figure 2-4: Yearly Structure for Sixth Grade

senting a 10-page list of possible titles, I thought it would be more helpful to walk you through one year with specific books and student work so that my teaching would be more tangible. In this chapter, I have included the literature circle units for middle school that I used this past year. Figures 2-4, 2-5, and 2-6 show the themes and topics that I have used in sixth, seventh, and eighth grades, respectively. The list changes each year as I shift titles, add new books, or change themes. Naturally, you will want to modify these ideas to fit your curriculum and grade level as well as the needs and interests of your particular group of students and the availability of books.

There are many other excellent young adult titles that can be used in literature circles. Appendix B includes additional titles and literature circle themes. The books in these lists also

Books	Skills and Strategies
Unit: Yukon Gold Rush (whole-class books)	

Jason's Gold by Will Hobbs	• Literature circle structure
	   Discussions
	   Journals
	• Point of view
	• Compare and contrast
	• Author's purpose
	• Simile

Unit: World War II (whole-class book)	
Goodnight, Mr. Tom by Michelle Magorian	• Plot structure • Dialect • Vocabulary (context clues)
Unit: Asian Culture and History (choice of books)	
Red Scarf Girl by Ji Ling Jiang *So Far From the Bamboo Grove* by Yoko Kawashima Watkins	• Characterization • Setting • Compare and contrast
Unit: Coming of Age (whole-class book)	
The Outsiders by S. E. Hinton	• Conflict • Author's style • Irony
Unit: Topic: Struggles of Young Mexican Immigrants (choice of books)	
Lupita Mañana by Patricia Beatty *Esperanza Rising* by Pam Muñoz Ryan *The Circuit* by Francisco Jiménez	• Vocabulary (context clues) • Voice • Metaphor

Figure 2-5: Yearly Structure for Seventh Grade

make great read-alouds or suggestions for students' independent reading. All of the titles mentioned in this book, including those in Appendix B, can also be found in the database on
the accompanying CD-ROM.

Books	Skills and Strategies
Unit: Survival and Friendship (whole-class book)	

The Maze by Will Hobbs	• Literature circle structure
	    Discussions
	    Journals
	• Literary devices
	• Inferences
	• Symbolism

Unit: Coming of Age (choice of books)	
Ironman by Chris Crutcher *When Zachary Beaver Came to Town* by Kimberly Willis Holt *Shabanu* by Suzanne Fisher Staples *The Maestro* by Tim Wynne-Jones	• Literary devices • Symbolism • Irony
Unit: Author Study of Paul Fleischmann (choice of books)	
Seedfolks *Whirligig* *Mind's Eye* *Saturnalia* *Seek*	• Author's style • Multiple voices • Plot structure
Unit: Slavery (whole-class book)	

Nightjohn and *Sarny* by Gary Paulsen	• Literary elements
	    Descriptive writing
	• Literary writing
	    Imagery
	• Characterization

Unit: Shakespeare (choice of books)	

The Shakespeare Stealer by Gary
  Blackwood
King of Shadows by Susan Cooper
Elizabeth I by Kathryn Lasky
Mary, Bloody Mary by Carolyn Meyer
	• Genre
	    Historical fiction
	• Time changes
	• Dialect
	• Setting
	• Characterization

Figure 2.6: Yearly Structure for Eighth Grade

Successful literature circles in middle school rely on good
books and effective organization. You have to set up a structure that works while also staying out of the way. Too much
teacher direction, and my students will chafe at the con-

straints. Too little direction, and they'll just skim the surface or erupt into chaos. The framework that I've described in this chapter provides support for discussions, written response, and artistic extensions. With effective support in place, anything is possible.

Chapter 3

Choosing Books

Mrs. King, be sure when you read this, you don't have anything else you have to do for awhile. Because once you start, you're not going to want to stop.

—Hillary, Grade 8

Literature circles live and die on the quality of the books students read. By middle school, many students are strong readers with well-developed tastes and the stamina to stick with a book to the end. Some are what I call "tenuous readers"— hanging on to their motivation to read by a slender thread. Still other students struggle with the mechanics and need support to build their confidence as readers. Literature circles have great power to pull students back into a love of reading when the motivational threads begin to shred and to open up the possibilities of books to struggling readers. But you have to have good books.

Choosing Good Books

To get to know each student as a reader, I begin the year with a survey adapted from the Reading-Writing Survey in Linda

Rief's *Seeking Diversity* (1992, p. 270). Students' responses provide information about their attitudes toward reading, as well as their interests, favorite books, and authors. From this survey, I also gain a sense of how much reading each student does at home.

I also ask my students what makes a good book. We continue this conversation throughout the year as we encounter new genres, authors, styles, and topics. Although it's easy to find criteria for book selection in every children's and adolescent literature textbook, I pay attention to the qualities that emerge as my students and I talk about the books we are reading.

Some of the most important considerations I keep in mind as I select books to use for literature circles are as follows:

- Does the book have depth, engagement, and content appropriate for young adults?

- Book appeal: Is it a "grabber" or "stretcher"?

- How much background knowledge will students need?

- How difficult is the text (e.g., length and format, use of dialect, vocabulary, concept density)?

- Do characters represent a diversity of backgrounds and experiences?

- Is there a balance of genders?

- Is there a variety of genres?

- Does a book fit with other parts of the curriculum?

Depth, Engagement, and Appropriate Content

Most important of all, books need enough "meat" to warrant close reading. I look for books with action to keep students interested and issues that are important to young people, such as becoming independent, taking responsibility for one's actions, and understanding others. By middle school, students are searching for books that reflect their internal conflicts and struggles, so I include books in which characters face challenges and serious issues, such as homelessness, injustice, survival, or belonging. One of the best examples is *Shabanu*

(Staples, 1989), for its captivating portrayal of a young girl's struggle against cultural expectations. To me, it is important to use books that end with hope. For many students, this widening of their world must be handled gently. For instance, I've found that books like *Parrot in the Oven* (Martinez, 1996) and *The Chocolate War* (Cormier, 1974) are too depressing for many middle school students and may be more appropriate in high school classes.

Many middle school students jump directly from children's literature into adult fiction, bypassing young adult books. Parents unfamiliar with more developmentally appropriate choices available in young adult literature often guide their children to novels by authors such as John Grisham and Tom Clancy, which often have questionable content and adult characters. I see this as an opportunity to inform parents about the plethora of enticing, high-quality young adult literature that is more appropriate for middle school readers.

Book Appeal

Sam Sebesta, a well-known expert in children's literature, describes books as either "grabbers" or "stretchers." A "grabber" is a book that students pick up independently because of the title, the topic, or the cover. *The Outsiders* (Hinton, 1967) is a perfect example of a book that, despite the fact that it was written 35 years ago, still proves a resounding favorite with middle school students. They are naturally drawn to the updated cover, the topic, the age of the protagonists, and the issues. "Stretchers" are books that students usually wouldn't discover on their own. For example, few of my students would pick *The Shakespeare Stealer* (Blackwood, 1998) at first glance. When we read the book in literature circles, however, this is one I hear my students discussing in the hallway and recommending to others.

Background Knowledge

One of the best qualities of young adult fiction is that it stretches adolescent readers into new territory. Sometimes, however, students need a roadmap for their literary journeys. Books such as *Red Scarf Girl* (Jiang, 1997) and *So Far From the Bamboo Grove* (Watkins, 1986) provide demanding reading, but students can be successful with classroom support and modeling. Focus lessons on point of view, conflict, and character development, along with related nonfiction materials about the time period and political issues, can give students the tools and background information they need to comprehend and appreciate these novels.

Text Difficulty

As the repertoire of young adult book choices expands in middle school, I often encounter books that have challenging text features such as dialect and unconventional organization. For example, the English country dialect in *Goodnight, Mr. Tom* (Magorian, 1981) lends authenticity to the text but can be confusing for my seventh-grade students. With added support, students can successfully navigate their way through and even learn to enjoy this new language. One strategy that works well is a word wall where students list unusual or descriptive words from the book. By the time we finish the book, I often hear these words popping up in students' speech or writing.

Monster by Walter Dean Myers (1999) is written as a screenplay about a boy on trial for murder. Both the format and topic proved too challenging for my sixth-grade readers. I now use this book in my eighth-grade class with much more success. Another book with an unconventional style is *Seek* by Paul Fleischman (2001). Written as a collage of voices heard by the main character, this book presents a challenge for even the most sophisticated eighth-grade readers. Students who choose it support one another as they make their way through the book. Students who are not ready to take on this challenge can choose one of the other titles.

Diversity

Books are both mirrors reflecting students' growing understanding of themselves and windows through which they view the world around them (Benson, 2000). When selecting books, I look for characters that will help my students to look inward—to examine their own feelings, actions, and challenges in light of others' experiences. I also search for characters, settings, issues, and themes that will expose my students to lives and insights quite different from their own.

For example, because it is set in contemporary Pakistan, *Shabanu* (Staples, 1989) challenges my students' preconceptions of this part of the world. At the same time, the main character wrestles with issues my students also face, such as growing up, falling in love, leaving family, and testing limits. Books like *Habibi* (Nye, 1997), *The Storyteller's Beads* (Kurtz, 1998), and *The Breadwinner* (Ellis, 2000) can help students make connections to current events in the Middle East and can spark conversations about values, family, and understanding among cultures.

Gender Balance

I also consider gender balance and interests of particular groups of students when selecting books. I'm always looking for books and authors like Gary Paulsen to entice reluctant middle school boys. He has made a specific effort to write for adolescent males.

> I was told not to write for boys. I said, "Why?" They said, "Because boys don't read. Girls read more. Write stories with girls in them." I said, "Why don't boys read?" "Well, there aren't any books." Ahh! I mean, the logic was incredible. (Paulsen, 1993)

Many contemporary young adult authors, such as Will Hobbs (*The Maze*, 1999) and Chris Crutcher (*Staying Fat for Sarah Byrnes*, 1993; *Whale Talk*, 2001), write with voice and conviction about issues and characters that ring true for both boys and girls. *The Outsiders* (Hinton, 1967) is another good example of a book that all my students enjoy. Even though the protagonists are all boys, the girls in my class relate to the theme of wanting to belong. I seek out books with both girls and boys as main characters that contain issues and themes that can cross gender lines. Sometimes these books can open the door to conversations about "Who am I?" and "Where do I belong?"

Genre Variety

In my language arts program as a whole, I believe it's important to expose students to a wide variety of genres, such as nonfiction, realistic fiction, poetry, historical fiction, biography, and fantasy. Many students become absorbed in one specific genre and miss out on other great reading opportunities. For example, many adolescents are not drawn to historical fiction, yet books like *Mary, Bloody Mary* (Meyer, 1999) and *Beware, Princess Elizabeth* (Meyer, 2001) have sparked some lively literature circle discussions.

I encourage students to try out different types of books by including different genres in the literature circle units. I also nudge students to expand their literary horizons in their independent reading. Each week, 3 or 4 students give a 5-minute book talk on their independent reading choices. They include bibliographic information, a short summary, and a personal reaction and evaluation. Students read a short passage to entice other students to want to read the book.

Curricular Match

When possible, I also select books to support the content taught in students' science and social studies classes, such as *Red Scarf Girl* (Jiang, 1997) and *So Far From the Bamboo Grove* (Watkins, 1986), which tie into the study of Asian cultures in seventh grade. However, I don't base all my selections on content area curriculum, because I don't make curriculum choices in those areas. If you do teach as part of a content area block, this would be an ideal way to integrate subjects. Instead, I choose several big issues, such as injustice, and spend several weeks reading and talking about this theme in relation to historical time periods.

Keeping Up With New Books

It takes energy and time to keep up with new books, so I rely on several main sources of support:

- Gathering recommendations from students
- Gathering recommendations from colleagues

- Searching for new books in libraries and bookstores
- Reading reviews in professional journals
- Looking for books online
- Reading on my own

Students are my best resource for new books. I ask them for suggestions and take notes when they share titles during their Friday Book Talks. I also pay attention as books are passed from student to student.

I get additional ideas from colleagues, whether they're next door or around the world. I seek out knowledgeable people at my local library and bookstore who can help point out new books that are popular with adolescents. I build book lists from titles recommended in professional books on literature circles. Finally,

---

Professional Books

Barbieri, Maureen. (1995). *Sounds From the Heart: Learning to Listen to Girls.* Portsmouth, NH: Heinemann.

Harris, Violet J. (Ed.). (1997). *Using Multiethnic Literature in the K–8 Classroom.* Norwood, MA: Christopher-Gordon.

Hill, Bonnie Campbell, Schlick Noe, Katherine L., & Johnson, Nancy J. (2001). *Literature Circles Resource Guide.* Norwood, MA: Christopher-Gordon. (Booklists and database on the CD-ROM.)

Hill, Bonnie Campbell, Johnson, Nancy J., & Schlick Noe, Katherine L. (Eds.). (1995). *Literature Circles and Response.* Norwood, MA: Christopher-Gordon.

Trelease, Jim. (1993). *Read All About It! Great Read-Aloud Stories, Poems, and Newspaper Pieces for Preteens and Teens.* NY: Penguin.

Professional Journals

Book Links (imprint of the American Library Association)
http://www.ala.org/BookLinks

The Horn Book
http://www.hbook.com

Middle School Journal (National Middle School Association)
http://www.nmsa.org/services/midjournal.htm

The Reading Teacher and *Journal of Adolescent and Adult Literacy* (International Reading Association)
http://www.reading.org/publications

Voices from the Middle (National Council of Teachers of English)
http://www.ncte.org/journals/

Figure 3-1: Professional Resources for Finding Books

when I read book reviews or articles on young adult literature in journals such as *Voices from the Middle*, *Book Links*, and *Middle School Journal*, I keep an eye out for titles that fit my literature circle themes or author focus (Figure 3-1).

Looking for New Books Online

The Internet has been a great source for books—especially when I need a good title but it's 11 p.m., the libraries and bookstores are closed, and my students are all tucked in bed. The vast information available on the Internet is also its greatest challenge. Therefore, I rely on several key sites where I know I'll get useful information for my classes (Figure 3-2).

The ALAN Review
Assembly on Literature for Adolescents of NCTE
http://scholar.lib.vt.edu/ejournals/ALAN/

American Library Association: Young Adult Library Services Association (YALSA)
http://www.ala.org/yalsa/booklists/index.html

Children's Literature Web Guide
http://www.acs.ucalgary.ca/~dkbrown

Database of Award Winning Children's Literature
http://www.dawcl.com

International Reading Association: Young Adults' Choices
http://www.reading.org/choices/

Literature Circles Resource Center
http://fac-staff.seattleu.edu/kschlnoe/LitCircles

Figure 3-2: Web Site Resources

Reading on My Own

Even with all of these great resources, I still rely mostly on my own reading to find the best books for my classes. Although I know literature circles can work even if I haven't read every book, I make the effort so that I'll know what my students are experiencing. In my classroom, everyone reads during independent reading time—including me. This is my chance to try out good literature circle books. Before we begin a new unit, I revisit the books I've read to look for teaching points or potential areas that may cause confusion. I also use Post-it® notes to mark significant passages or places where I may want to focus on a specific literary element or literary device (Figure 3-3).

Figure 3-3: Preparing for Literature Circles

Obtaining Multiple Copies

Finding enough copies of high-quality books is always a challenge when you begin literature circles. When I structure units around broad themes, I find that I have a wider range of books from which to choose. If you can collect a few book sets each year, your collection will slowly expand. I usually add one new set each year or replace a title that was less successful with a more engaging or more recent book. Until you build a collection, you may want to start by selecting short stories from an anthology or begin with one whole-class novel. When you're ready to search for multiple copies of a single title, you can check your school and public libraries or your school book room. Below are a few additional recommendations.

Bonus Points

One of the best methods to build your collection of book sets is to use bonus points from book orders. The book companies carry the latest releases at reduced prices or free with bonus points.

Book Exchange

Another way I expand my book collection is to host a "book exchange" with teachers at my school. All the middle school teachers bring lists of novels they own in multiple copies. We check for duplications across grade levels and swap titles we think are inappropriate for our students for ones that are a better match. When I taught sixth grade with another teacher, we each collected books for two units for our own classroom, then exchanged our units midyear.

"Wish List"

Every spring our school hosts a book fair. Each teacher creates a "wish list" that is posted at the cashier's desk. Generous parents who want to contribute to their own student's classroom library can donate books for literature circles. Families have also donated books in place of treats to honor students' birthdays and to commemorate holidays.

Selecting Different Books for Different Grades

When selecting literature circle books, I also consider the developmental needs and interests of different grade levels. Sixth graders often respond at a more literal level, and I often find that books with more explicit themes and more action, such as *Roll of Thunder, Hear My Cry* (Taylor, 1976), are more successful with this age group. One year I tried using *The Maestro* (Wynne-Jones, 1996) for literature circles in seventh grade, but I found that the book was more successful with eighth graders, who could discuss the conflict between the father and son in more depth. The older students were able to delve into the tougher issues and to recognize subtleties of the characters' relationships and changes.

By the time students are in eighth grade, they are usually able to discuss more abstract ideas and concepts and can make inferences more easily. For example, Andy's journal entry highlights the symbolism in *When Zachary Beaver Came to Town* (Holt, 1999) when the characters release a swarm of ladybugs into the field:

This book has several climaxes. One was the releasing of the ladybugs. It is also known as the Ladybug Waltz, a tradition started by Wayne, Cal's older brother who died in the Viet Nam war. It summed up his life and was not only a way of releasing the ladybugs to protect the fields, but was a way of renewing the community and healing the pain and loss from Wayne's absence. This book was filled with loss and redemption. It made me realize that no matter how bad life can get, it will always get better.

When Zachary Beaver is made fun of that is demeaning and counter to his rights as a human being. I wonder if we are all trapped in the "trailers" of our own subconscious by our doubts and fears. All any of us need is someone to make us take some steps and the courage to step outside of our comfort zone.

Meeting the Needs of Less Proficient Readers

As I create themed literature units, I try to select books that represent a wide range of reading levels. This is one of the most challenging aspects of selecting books, and it highlights the importance of choosing a broad theme. I make sure that I select at least one book in each unit that has intrinsic high interest and plenty of action to hook the more struggling readers. When I booktalk the choices for each literature circle set, I honestly state which books will be "quick reads" and which ones might present more of a challenge because of length, vocabulary, or assumed background knowledge. To become independent readers, students need to learn how to choose books that work for them. I know I'm giving students a perfect opportunity to practice this skill when I allow them to select their own books for literature circles.

When possible, I also try to purchase books on tape or ask volunteers to read the book onto a tape. For some students, listening to a book read aloud can enable them to participate more fully during literature discussions. These students may also find it helpful to read the book aloud with a resource teacher or reading specialist. At other times, students may read the book or portions of the book with volunteers, family members, or a peer.

Over the years I have found that being part of a literature circle discussion can motivate students to persevere through a challenging text. Similarly, taking part in the discussion often increases their comprehension. The goal is to help every student take part as a valued member of the reading community.

My Secret Weapon: The Read-Aloud

I read aloud to all of my middle school classes. This is everyone's favorite part of the day. An indispensable part of my entire language arts program—truly, my secret weapon— the read-aloud accomplishes so much. As I read aloud, I model enjoyment of reading and take advantage of moment-to-moment opportunities to talk about characters, language, author's style—everything I want students to understand about literature. All of this happens during an enjoyable experience that no one wants to end.

Reading a book aloud also helps to create a sense of community within the class and provides a shared reference point. I sometimes choose books to launch or support literature circles. For example, I often read aloud *Chive* (Barre, 1993) during the unit on homelessness. At other times, I select a book that I know students will enjoy, such as *Stargirl* (Spinelli, 2000), *Tangerine* (Bloor, 1997), or *Stand Tall* (Bauer, 2002) that touch upon issues of growing up and conformity. I use the read-alouds to model fluency and expression and to reinforce focus lessons I've taught during literature circles. For example, if we're learning about similes and metaphors in our literature circle books, I make sure to point out examples I come across as I read aloud.

There are enough high-quality books to fuel middle school literature circles from now into the next century. In this chapter, I've included some of the most thought-provoking and response-laden titles that have proved successful with my students. Further suggestions are included in Appendix B and in the database on the accompanying CD-ROM. I also recommend that you check the resources presented earlier in this chapter. In addition to recommendations by my students and colleagues, the professional books, journals, and Web sites that I list are my key resources for finding fabulous books.

Chapter 4

Supporting Quality Discussions

Discussions are important because especially now, with hormones, everyone disagrees, but if you bring in a good book, all of a sudden, they agree!

—Ian, Grade 6

Discussions are really the heart and soul of literature circles—the key element that sets literature circles apart from other methods of teaching. When my students talk about what they have read, they take charge of their own learning. They choose what they talk about and learn new viewpoints from one another. Because middle school students love to socialize, this way of learning comes naturally. With some structured guidance, students learn listening skills and the art of good conversation.

Benefits of Discussions

Through discussions, students try out their own thinking while learning from one another. Morgan, one of my seventh graders, put it very succinctly when she said, "I learned about other people's views of the book. That seemed to open a new door of thought on my part." Discussions offer the following benefits:

- Encouraging natural response
- Deepening understanding
- Building on students' natural desire to talk
- Exposing students to different viewpoints or reactions
- Providing opportunity for student choice
- Encouraging students to take responsibility for their own learning
- Providing positive modeling by peers
- Developing listening and speaking skills

As explained in chapter 2, students usually meet for discussions two or three times during the course of a literature circle unit. During the early conversations as they begin a new book, students come to know the characters and often help each other to clarify the setting. This is also a good time to begin making predictions. In the middle of the book, students can once again check their understanding by comparing their thoughts with other members of the group. For instance, they may talk about the evolving plot, make connections to their own lives and other books, and examine how the author builds suspense and uses foreshadowing. During the final discussion at the end of the book, students often share their opinions, check initial predictions, and talk about the author's style.

Providing Guidance for Discussions

Of course, all of this doesn't just happen. I discovered this the first time I tried literature circles several years ago. After dividing all my students into groups of 5, I sent them off to talk about their independent reading books. I figured that if I just told them to talk about their books, they would. The result was chaos. Several factors contributed to the disaster. Because the students hadn't all read the same book, they had no common frame of reference. Instead of interacting in a dynamic conversation, they engaged in show-and-tell. I had also simply assumed that they would know how to talk, so I had spent no time showing them how or clarifying my expectations. After reading some books about literature circles and talking to several colleagues, I decided to try again, this time with a plan.

Effective discussions require guidance and experience. I must first establish an atmosphere of safety and comfort in my classroom so that students feel free to express their ideas and feelings. Students also need a schema for discussion, a mental image of what they're striving to replicate. Finally, students need to develop the social skills of conversation before they'll be able to participate as thoughtful and effective contributors.

Creating a Climate of Trust

Students will open up and talk honestly about books only in a climate of trust in which everyone's opinion is honored. Students need to learn to listen, to invite others to share their thoughts, and to disagree respectfully. The challenge inevitably arises about equal participation in a discussion. Some students tend to dominate a conversation, whereas others rarely contribute. As a class, we brainstorm ways to include all voices in a discussion and how to draw in quiet participants. I have found that shy students sometimes just need time to develop trust before they are willing to speak up. At other times, students need an invitation, such as "Malika, we haven't heard from you yet. What do you think?"

One year, I had a sixth grader who rarely contributed during literature circles. No amount of prodding or questioning would bring more than a one-word response from her. Midway through the year, she came to a discussion emotionally energized by her book, *A Place to Call Home* (Koller, 1995). The conversation was very sedate until she ranted for a full minute about the injustices the main character was experiencing. Her group listened intently, realizing what a breakthrough this was. When she finished speaking and they recovered from their shock, her whole group stood and applauded. Watching her face, I could tell that she knew this was a compliment. She had gained their respect with her input—when she was ready.

Modeling Discussions

The most successful way I have found to communicate discussion goals to my students is a technique called a "fishbowl." Nothing is more powerful than a live discussion. Through my own observations and information from the previous year's teachers, I select five students who I think can model a good discussion for their peers. I ask if they would be willing to take part in a small-group discussion in front of the class. Because this modeling occurs at the beginning of literature circles, we use the first whole class novel. I give each student three Post-it® notes and ask them to mark their favorite spot, a question they have, and a particularly descriptive quote from the book. These serve as tools for students to gather at least three ideas they can share during the discussion.

Here's how the fishbowl worked last year in my sixth-grade class. Once we finished reading *Song of the Trees* (Taylor, 1975), five students sat in front of the class in a semicircle and pretended the rest of us weren't there (Figure 4-1). I instructed the audience to observe and take notes, identifying what made this discussion work well, and listing some things that might improve the conversation. Then we all sat back and listened.

Figure 4-1: Fishbowl Discussion

After about 10 minutes, I asked the students in the audience to share their observations, which I recorded on a chart, "What Makes a Good Discussion?" Students contributed the following observations:

- Everyone contributed.
- Everyone came prepared with ideas to discuss.
- When one person brought up a topic, other students asked questions or shared their own ideas about the same topic.
- They referred back to the book, reading bits from the text.

When asked what could make the discussion flow even more smoothly, students pointed out the following:

- Sometimes several people spoke at once instead of listening.
- Not everyone contributed equally. Some people need to talk more.
- They switched topics so fast that they never talked about any one thing long enough.
- They seemed to just tell their own ideas rather than get into a conversation about each other's ideas.

We added these ideas to the chart after rewording them as positive guidelines. We continually add to this chart and refer to it throughout the year.

Another way to provide modeling is to videotape an effective discussion. The advantage of this technique is that you can literally "pause" the conversation to discuss what works and what could be improved. Because we've built a climate of respect and safety in our classroom, students aren't afraid to offer or receive these critiques. Once we have debriefed after a fishbowl or videotaped conversation, students need a chance to tackle their own discussions.

Building Social Skills

Some students come to middle school with a well-developed understanding of the give and take of conversations. They can rely on their natural skills of diplomacy to insert their ideas into a discussion and to invite others to take part. Others may need some help. We work on fine-tuning social graces in all contexts, but it is through literature circles that students most clearly see the need to put those skills to work. I address social skills through focus lessons and debriefings so that students understand the characteristics of a good discussion.

The chart in Figure 4-2 is adapted from a strategy I found in *Getting Started With Literature Circles* (Schlick Noe & Johnson, 1999). My students brainstormed specific behaviors they would see and hear during effective literature circle discussions. This chart becomes a focal point as I observe discussions and look for strategies I need to support through focus lessons. Because we've made these social skills explicit and concrete, my students gradually begin to exhibit the behaviors naturally during their discussions.

Discussion elements	What would you see?	What would you hear?
Active listening	*Eye contact* *Face speaker* *Leaning in* *Nodding head* *Focus*	*One voice at a time* *Soft voices*
Active participation *Respond to ideas* *Share feelings*	*Everyone contributes* *Stay on one topic at a time* *Be prepared*	*Respectful responses* *Build on others' ideas* *Positive comments* *Everyone's ideas accepted*
Supporting opinions with evidence	*Use books and Post-it® notes to support ideas* *Use journals*	*Use quotes as support* *Explain why*
Encouraging others	*Pull in quiet people* *Face speaker* *Nod head*	*Ask good questions* *Ask "What do you think?"* *Wait for people to finish* *Make sure everyone is heard*
Disagreeing constructively	*Eye contact* *Listen patiently*	*Respectful responses* *Explain your position or opinion* *Paraphrase others' ideas*

Figure 4-2: Discussion Etiquette

Beyond Role Sheets

In many classrooms, teachers use role sheets (Daniels, 1994) as part of the structure of literature circle discussions. However, I have found that students get hung up on the roles rather than responding to the text naturally. I don't want students to be constrained to a single role in a discussion. When I read *The Girl With the Pearl Earring* (Chevalier, 2001) in my adult book club, I would have hated being the Word Wizard. I wanted to talk about the symbolism of the girl's hair. By teaching strategies through focus lessons, my students can choose whether to share a passage, an interesting word, an illustration, or a question. The students and the books, not the roles, determine the type of response. In this way, students take the lead in responding to literature.

Preparing for a Discussion

While students read, they gather ideas to bring to the discussion. I want to give them quick ways to capture the ideas that will spark their conversations. However, I'm also careful to steer them away from extensive writing that they might be tempted to read aloud during the discussion. The purpose of the journal (described more fully in chapter 5) is to capture more reflective thinking on paper. During their discussions, I want my students to experience the flow of a real conversation. Therefore, I share three simple tools that help to jog students' memories without becoming burdensome.

Post-it® Notes

Post-it® notes are a great tool for discussions. They are small and relatively inexpensive, stick where you place them, and

Figure 4-3: Using Post-it® Notes

can be easily removed. At the beginning of a unit, I give each student a few notes to store in the inside cover of their literature circle book. When these are gone, students supplement with scraps of paper or Post-it® notes from home. Students use them to keep track of ideas, questions, favorite scenes, or anything else that stands out as they read (Figure 4-3). Because they are small, Post-it® notes offer a place to capture quick reminders for discussion.

Bookmarks

The main purpose of the bookmark is to record the weekly reading schedule (described in chapter 2). However, the blank back side also offers a convenient spot for informally jotting down ideas, "Golden Lines," questions, or interesting words for discussion (Figure 4-4). Early in the year, I introduce the concept of Golden Lines (Schlick Noe & Johnson, 1999) by sharing a variety of examples. I look for quotes with descriptive language, as well as powerful, emotion-charged writing. When students note the page number on their bookmarks, the group is more likely to turn back to the text to define a word or re-read a passage.

> Christine Jonston
>
> Esperanza Rising
> By Pam Muñez Ryan
> ☆ Premonition p.9
> ☆ Big pearls of blood pulsed from her thumb p.8
> ☆ Could you understand all of the Spanish in this book?
> ☆ Capricious p.13
> ☆ Cacaphony p.250
> ☆ Her smile faded, her chest tightened, and a heavy blanket of anguish smothered her smallest joy p.23

Figure 4-4: Bookmark

Discussion Ideas

As another discussion tool, I often ask students to record several specific ideas or questions in their journals. We talk about the characteristics of questions or conversation threads that will energize a discussion. Periodically, I elicit examples of successful questions from students' discussions, which we record on a chart, "Great Questions to Keep Your Conversation Going." Here are some questions that one of my sixth graders wanted to talk about when her group met to discuss *Homecoming* (Voigt, 1981):

- What do you think will happen in the sequel?
- Do you want to read it? Why?
- Why do you think the author included all these "rescuers" (Will, Claire, Stewart, Winky, etc.)? Do you like them?
- Do you think Dicey is right—do you only have a home when you die?
- Read pages 165 and 166, which show James's intelligence.
- Read pages 227 and 228, which are my favorite funny part.
- Would you change anything about this book?

When I look back over the passages she marked to share and the questions she raised, I can clearly see that her ideas are far more provocative than any list I might have handed out.

Students don't always need outside supports to help them find something interesting to say in their discussions. However, many students forget the great ideas that jumped off the page as they were reading. They often need some way to hang on to their thoughts long enough to share them in a discussion. Once introduced to a variety of tools to capture ideas for discussion, students often gravitate to one or two that they prefer. As long as students prepare for discussion in some way, I'm satisfied.

Developing Discussions Over Time

Looking back over my development as a teacher, my expectations and level of involvement have clearly changed over the years. I've moved from a high degree of teacher direction in my first experiences with literature circles to a more student-centered approach now that I have a better sense of what literature circles can do for students and what students can do with literature circles. However, every year is a new beginning. As I get to know each new group of students, I watch closely to detect their level of sophistication and experience with literature circles. I find that I fall back on more teacher direction when it is needed.

I characterize my progression from teacher-centered to student-centered discussions in three phases.

Phase 1: Teacher-Directed Groups

When I first started using literature circles in my classroom, I wasn't sure what would happen, so I had only one group meet at a time. The rest of the students read, wrote in their journals, or worked on a response project. The key to success at this phase was having clear expectations for students who were not participating in the discussion, and then teaching them how to work independently. Before each discussion, we reviewed the expectations, and I specified exactly what was and was not acceptable.

Although I rarely participated in the discussions, I sat adjacent to the group and listened to everything they said. This gave me ample assessment information on individual students, kept the students on track, and provided grist for debriefing sessions and focus lessons. They wouldn't talk about last weekend's soccer game while I was sitting there. For me, this was a comfortable place to start. I've summarized the advantages and disadvantages of Phase 1 in Figure 4-5.

Advantages
- Students stayed on track.
- I could intervene if the conversation stalled.
- Assessment was relatively easy. When I sat near the group, they ignored me and I could take anecdotal notes.

Disadvantages
- Because only one discussion took place a day, each group discussed different books, which made whole-class lessons and debriefing more challenging.
- Although I did not sit in with the groups, they still relied on me to help keep the conversation going.

Figure 4-5: Phase 1

Phase 2: Teacher-Facilitated Groups

As the students became more proficient and I felt more confident in their discussion abilities, I had two or three discussions going on at a time while I floated around the room listening and observing. My role was less as a director and more as a facilitator who stepped in only when needed to redirect, suggest new topics, or mediate disputes. At this stage, discussions lasted anywhere from 10 to 20 minutes as students developed the ability to sustain more in-depth discussion. Figure 4-6 lists the advantages and disadvantages of Phase 2.

Advantages
- Students began to develop their own discussion strategies and techniques.
- I was still in close enough proximity to gather assessment data and to make sure students stayed on track.
- Students were often more open with sharing their ideas when I was not around, because they didn't feel that every comment was being evaluated.

Disadvantages
- Students still discussed different parts of the book on different days, which made whole-class lessons and debriefing challenging.
- The noise level was sometimes distracting to the students who were not involved in a discussion, as well as to the other discussion groups. We had to work very hard to develop "six-inch voices" (a real challenge for middle school students). I had to constantly remind them to keep their voices low.

Figure 4-6: Phase 2

Phase 3: Student-Managed Groups

In my classroom now, the literature circle groups all meet at the same time. It's not unusual for discussions to last up to 30 minutes. This method means that I can roam the room and assess as I listen in on the conversations. Because we work hard on building discussion skills throughout the year, students can usually manage their own conversations quite well.

As I become more of an observer, I do more teaching before and after the discussions than I did in previous years. I believe it's important to make my expectations clear and to work with students to develop their independence. For example, students need a clear idea of acceptable noise levels—telling them to "keep it down" rarely works by itself. I draw a line on the board with noise levels gauged from "the lunchroom" to "silent reading time." Then I write "literature circles" closer to the latter. They soon learn to monitor the noise level in the classroom on their own.

I don't want students to keep on task and talk about the book just because I'm standing there. I want them to take ownership of their conversations. When a discussion doesn't go well, I hand the problem back over to the students by asking, "What can you do when the discussion gets off track?" I write down their ideas on a chart, which they can then refer to when the challenge arises. Now I often hear students urging others back to a relevant topic, and I don't miss my policing role a bit. The advantages and disadvantages of Phase 3 are shown in Figure 4-7.

Advantages
- All groups are talking at the same time.
- Scheduling is much easier.
- Students enjoy the independence and know they are being trusted.

Disadvantages
- The noise level can be very high. Students must continue to refine their awareness of appropriate volume.
- It is hard to listen in on every group. (The conversation may revert to soccer when I am across the room.)

Figure 4-7: Phase 3

Debriefing: The Key to Successful Discussions

Whether one group meets at a time or all groups meet at once, I have found that the number one key to success is to debrief after every discussion. As soon as the discussion is over, I ask students to reflect on what went well and what they could change to make their discussion go better next time (Figure 4-8). It helps students to feel in control; the ball is in their court and they're in charge of making these discussions work.

Figure 4-8: Debriefing

Sometimes I ask for a quick written comment in their journals; more often we debrief orally. If just one or two groups have met, I have this conversation with each group individually. When all the groups have their discussions at the same time, we will "unpack" our thoughts as a whole class. I ask each group to share a high point of their discussion, and I contribute my observations as well.

Here is a list from one group of students when I asked, "What are some things that went well in your discussion today?"

- Our group stayed on one topic for a while rather than just answering briefly and moving on.
- We talked about how we wouldn't want to be in Shabanu's shoes and how hard it would be if society dictated your life.
- We worked on not interrupting each other so that everyone could hear each person's ideas.
- We made connections to other books we've read.

I then asked, "What would you do differently next time?" and received these responses:

- We ran out of ideas to talk about, so we decided we should come with more ideas beforehand.
- Make sure that one person doesn't do all the talking and that everybody gets a chance to share their ideas.

- We got really frustrated when one person in our group told us he had read ahead and he blurted out the ending.

I took advantage of this last comment to discuss the purpose of reading the books in sections. When students stop at the same point, everyone can slow down and read more intensively rather than rushing through a book. I also addressed the challenge of overzealous talkers, and we brainstormed ways to respectfully balance the contributions of all group members. The debriefing process provides valuable feedback to my students and to me.

Focus Lessons for Discussions

I refine students' discussion skills through two main categories of focus lessons: one about the art of conversation and the other on understanding literature. Students' needs, the specific books, and my school and state guidelines drive the content and timing of these lessons. For example, when stu-

Figure 4-9: Focus Lesson

dents first start out, they need more guidance on the process of discussion. Later on, I begin to weave in focus lessons tied to curriculum guidelines for each grade level.

I also grab the teachable moments when they occur. For example, when I see students struggling with a certain component of quality discussions, I will take the opportunity to address that particular issue. When students read a book that has excellent examples of similes and metaphors, then I will focus my lessons on these elements of literature.

Below is a list of some of the focus lessons I have used in the past to support quality discussions. They evolve from what I observe during discussions, as well as what I know from past experience that students need to learn. They are as follows:

- Coming prepared for a discussion
- Starting a conversation
- Taking turns naturally
- Inviting quiet people into the discussion
- Listening empathetically
- "Piggybacking" off other people's ideas
- Disagreeing politely
- Backing up opinions with specific examples from the book
- Rescuing a flagging conversation
- Using Golden Lines to discuss the author's style

Below is a list of some of the focus lessons I use to promote a better understanding of literature. Again, I plan lessons based on my students' strengths and needs as readers and writers. I also glean ideas from professional books, such as *Strategies that Work* (Harvey & Goudvis, 2000) and *Yellow Brick Roads* (Allen, 2000). Sample focus lessons include:

- Making predictions with supporting evidence from the text
- Analyzing characters and their motivations
- Recognizing the importance of setting
- Determining the theme
- Analyzing plot structure, including conflict, climax, and resolution
- Discussing author's purpose, craft, and use of language
- Noticing imagery, simile, metaphor, and irony
- Connecting events and characters to other books, movies, or personal experiences
- Recognizing the characteristics of various genres

Teacher Evaluation

Discussions give me a great way to assess my students' developing knowledge and skills. However, I simply can't keep all that information in my head. Over the years, I've developed a way to use anecdotal notes to assess students' participation, attitude, and comprehension during literature circle discussions.

Anecdotal Notes

I keep a clipboard with a grid of rectangles that fit 1½ x 2 inch Post-it® notes for each class. Each student's name is permanently recorded above a square so I can use this sheet over and over again. I place blank Post-it® notes on the grid ahead of time so that I only have to record the date and the student's comments or contributions. Once I have collected comments for each of my students, I transfer the sticky notes onto individual sheets that I keep in my Teacher Notebook (Hill, Ruptic, & Norwick, 1998), where I gather information on each student throughout the year.

Anecdotal Records for: 7th Grade Language Arts			
Patti	**Anne**	**Bob**	**Tony**
10/7 • frequent ④ contributions • notes 1st person point of view • elaborates on Ted's comment re: author's style	10/7 • asks for help ③ "what happened to Willie in apt?" • reads passage that confused her • asks "fat" questions	10/7 • Analyzes mom's ④ character • Discusses author's choice of point of view • Connections between mom & son	10/7 • has not read all pages • unable to contribute much ②
Sam	**Kelsey**	**Nathan**	**Teresa**
10/7 • asks others -favorite character? -favorite part? • separate conversation with Jason ②	10/7 • behind in reading • seem confused by turn in plot ②	10/7 • sustains discussion ④ w/insightful Q's • brings up unusual words • symbolism - change in Willie, Tom & war	10/7 • listens actively • points out slow pace of plot in beginning • tracks changes in Willie ③
Grace	**Ted**	**Jason**	**Emily**
10/7 • confused by chain of events in apt. • "aha!" when Jacob explains ③ • predicts outcome of Willie's predicament	10/7 • leads discussion • pulls in Susan w/question • author's style ④	10/7 • yawning /disengaged • no book • talks w/Sam ½ group ①	10/7 • shares opinion ③ of main characters • looks up word when no one can figure it out • discusses cover

Figure 4-10: Anecdotal Notes for the Class

Discussions contribute 25 percent toward students' final reading grade, which I base on my anecdotal notes. As I listen to the groups, I score each student's contributions holistically. I use the same 4-point scale for discussions as I do for journals (chapter 5) and extension projects (chapter 6). Figure 4-10 shows my anecdotal notes from a group's discussion of *Goodnight, Mr. Tom* (Magorian, 1981).

A 1 or 2 signifies that students are either uninvolved, unprepared, or seldom contribute to the discussion. For example, I noted that Jason was "yawning and disengaged," had "no book," and "talks with Sam instead of group." I give a 3 to students who share a variety of ideas and build on others' comments. You can see that Emily shared her opinion, talked about the book's cover, and used a dictionary to define a new word for the group. The notes I took about Nathan's contribution show what I look for when I give a 4: a more advanced understanding of the book and the ability to sustain a discussion with insightful comments. Because students meet for discussions three times as they read a novel, I try to record one or two Post-it® notes for each student for one literature circle unit.

These observations are directly linked to the focus lessons I have taught. I share some of my notes during the debriefing in order to build upon the positive discussion strategies I observed. These anecdotal notes also are an invaluable source of information for evaluation and narrative comments at conferences and on report cards.

My anecdotal notes frequently lead to new focus lessons. For example, during a discussion in my seventh-grade class, I noticed that some students threw themselves into the discussion, whereas others sat back and "rode along." I knew I wasn't the only one who picked up on this when one student flatly stated, "Mark, you need to say something." I made note of this on my clipboard. During the post-discussion debriefing, I alluded to that blunt response by sharing my observation that some students were contributing much more than others. I asked, "What would be a tactful way to pull in quiet members of your group?" During a focus lesson the next week, I followed up by mentioning that I would watch to see how well each group tried to include everyone in the discussions. Equal participation became the target that day. In this way, my anecdotal notes provide concrete examples I can share with students after each discussion. As we build on what's working well and identify what could be better, the discussions improve over time.

When I have other adults in the classroom, I often ask them to listen in to groups and to record their own observations using anecdotal notes (Figure 4-11). Volunteers, student teachers, assistants, librarians, ESL teachers, or reading specialists can sometimes provide another pair of eyes and another perspective. Taking anecdotal notes is easy and helps these adults to feel valuable and useful in the classroom. They also enjoy being trusted with this responsibility and the opportunity to be actively involved. When appropriate, I ask volunteers to read *Taking Note* (Power, 1996) to help them understand the purpose of this assessment strategy as well as to provide ideas about what to write down. In addition, I give them a list of specific target behaviors to look for (Hill, Ruptic, and Norwick, 1998, p. 262). During the debriefing, the guests are asked to share any insights or observations. The information they record becomes part of my assessment of discussion.

Figure 4-11: Adult Volunteer Taking Anecdotal Notes

Student Self-Evaluation

I expect my middle school students to take charge of their own learning. I don't want them to passively wait for me to give them a grade. My goal is to involve them in the assessment process so that they can evaluate their own work, acknowledge what they do well, and set goals for themselves before they head off to high school. As students become more adept at analyzing their own learning, their self-evaluation contributes valuable information to help me plan instruction and to guide students' ongoing growth. I incorporate two types of student self-evaluation of discussions: rubrics early in the year and written reflections in journals on an ongoing basis.

Rubrics

At the beginning of the school year, I use a "Discussion Rubric" adapted from *Classroom Based Assessment* (Hill, Ruptic, & Norwick, 1998) to ease into self-evaluation and reinforce my expectations for discussions (Figure 4-12). Immediately after an early discussion, I hand out the rubric and ask students to fill it out. Students keep these rubrics in their reading journals and refer to them before their next meeting.

DISCUSSION RUBRIC

Name: _____ Date: _____

Check the boxes that apply to this discussion, then mark an "X" in the top bar to indicate approximate placement on a continuum. Use the back for comments: what you noticed as strengths and weaknesses, and what you found interesting and unique.

1	2	3	4
☐ Not prepared for discussion	☐ Brings book and discussion tools	☐ Brings book with a few passages marked	☐ Brings book with many passages marked
☐ Rarely contributes ideas to discussion	☐ Contributes ideas to discussions occasionally or when prompted	☐ Contributes ideas appropriately to discussions	☐ Contributes significantly to discussion
☐ Conversation off-task or does not contribute	☐ Difficulty keeping discussion going	☐ Generally keeps the discussion going	☐ Effectively keeps the discussion going
☐ Rarely listens or responds to group members	☐ Sometimes listens and responds appropriately, occasionally asks questions or shares ideas	☐ Listens and responds adequately (occasionally reads unclear passages, discusses unknown words, asks questions, listens actively, builds on others' comments, makes connections to other books and experiences, discusses author's style and literary elements)	☐ Listens and responds thoughtfully (consistently reads unclear passages, discusses unknown words, asks questions, listens actively, builds on others' comments, makes connections to other books and experiences, discusses author's style and literary elements)

Figure 4-12: Discussion Rubric

Comments:

Written Reflection After Discussions

Once or twice during each literature circle unit, I ask students to reflect in writing on their discussion. For example, after the eighth graders read *The Maze* (Hobbs, 1999), Rachel wrote the following response in her journal:

> Today in my group, we talked about the likes and dislikes about *The Maze.* We made comments about favorite characters and the setting. We also tried putting ourselves in Rick's (the main character's) position. I also learned that Will Hobbs writes books from his own experiences.

Through these entries, I sometimes learn about problems that arose during a discussion, such as when Morgan wrote:

> It became somewhat frustrating to me that one of the people in my group did not contribute at all. This person only said a few words during the whole discussion. The discussion would have probably been better if the other person could have contributed more to the group and given more of their personal insights on the story. Hopefully, next time the person will be more inclined to talk.

I responded by writing in Morgan's journal, "This is challenging. What are some ways that you and other group members could draw that person in?" I also brought up this challenge as a focus lesson prior to the next literature circle, and the class brainstormed ways to bring quiet members into the discussion. This is a perfect example of how assessment can guide instruction. If a student mentions a problem in his or her journal that doesn't come up during the discussion debriefing, I will try to address the issue anonymously in my observations to the class. That way, I can facilitate problem solving even when students are reluctant to air problems in public on their own.

Figure 4-13 shows Kate's reflections about what she's doing well and how she hopes to improve.

Discussion Evaluation

Name: Kate Haller   Date: 9/26/01

What things am I doing well in my literature circle?

I contribute questions and conversation starters. I am a good listener and try to encourage others. I respond to prompts from others and stay on top of the reading.

What things could I do to help my literature circle go better?

I could come more prepared by marking spots to talk about. I could also work on having a question ready when the conversation dies and staying on the discussion topic.

Figure 4-13: Discussion Evaluation

Goal Setting

Self-evaluation is not easy for everyone. It requires a high level of metacognition and self-awareness and is a skill that must be nurtured and refined. Effective self-evaluation is directly connected to successful learning. Therefore, I try to guide students to use their growing awareness of their own growth to set realistic goals. I ask students to record these goals in their journals along with one or two concrete steps they could take to accomplish their goals. Ashley wrote, "I'm starting conversations and keeping them going. I also think that I contributed some good points to the discussion." For her goal, she suggested honestly, "I could not go off subject and if someone does, return them to the conversation. I also think I should not be as bossy as I am sometimes!"

Students periodically revisit their goals and reflect upon them in writing. Kelsey, an eighth grader, wrote the following:

> Today I helped clear up understandings about certain passages, asked questions and answered questions to keep the discussion going. I listened to everyone's thoughts, ideas, and questions. I added my opinions and answered questions to clear things up. I also contributed to our discussion of the author's craft. Next time I would compare the book to other books I've read!

My Own Goal for Discussions

I have just one goal for discussions, and it's a big one: I would like my students to find the same joy in talking about books that I experience in my adult book club, where people are bursting to get their ideas out and to learn more from others' insights. I know that the first step is to provide the best books possible, so I continue to seek out books that my students can't put down. Modeling my own reading is also critical. I know that the more students take ownership for literature circles, the more invested they'll be in making their discussions meaningful and engaging, more closely resembling the conversations I envision for them.

Monica, one of my seventh-grade students, told me, "I enjoy having discussions with my classmates. I like to know other people's views of the story. Sometimes I understand the book more after talking about it." Another student quietly admitted, "Discussions are personally good for me since I'm a little shy. It helps me get used to the idea of speaking in front of people." As I watch my students discuss books in literature circles, I'm amazed at what they'll let me—and each other— know about what they think and feel. As they talk, I can see their growth as readers, writers, and young adults take shape in front of me.

Chapter 5 ⤠

Supporting Quality
Written Response

*Journals are one of my favorite things about this
style of teaching. It gives us a chance to give a more
in-depth answer to why we like or dislike the book.*

—Cody, Grade 8

During a discussion, all those great ideas float off into the air.
Unless I'm sitting there taking notes, those insights disappear
once they're spoken. I think of writing as "planned thinking"
that can be seized, examined, and revisited. Through writing,
students capture their thinking over time, so that they—and
I—can see clear evidence of their growth. I want students to
listen in on their own thinking. I don't think they naturally
stop to think about what they're reading *as* they're reading,
but writing forces them to slow down, allowing that inner
voice to be heard. The writer can look back and erase, rethink, and try again another way.

Figure 5-1: Student Response Journal

Purpose of Written Response

In literature circles in my classroom, writing serves three main purposes. First, when students "think aloud on paper," only one person can "talk" at a time, allowing for more thoughtful, in-depth "conversation." Writing is private and personal. Therefore, some students are more willing to take risks and articulate their feelings on paper than they are in discussions.

Second, writing forces students to pause momentarily to reflect on character development and interactions and the events that have taken place. Students deepen their capacity to read and think critically by writing down some of their thoughts.

Third, written response nurtures student "self talk" (Benson, 2002). Responding to prompts such as, "I think...," "I feel...," or "I wonder..." encourages students to think more deeply about the book and to make personal connections with characters and events. The prompts provide a bridge as students learn to talk to themselves as they read.

I also find that students become more analytical in their writing than they do during discussions. They seem to feel less inhibited and are more able to let their thoughts flow. As they write, they often reread passages in the text and reread their own written responses. This often leads students to re-consider their opinions and look for further evidence.

Different Ways to Use Writing

Through writing, my students translate their thinking into permanent form. Therefore, it's an effective tool before and after discussions and as part of the debriefing process.

Before Discussion

It's helpful to have students use journals to sort out what they want to talk about before they meet. I often ask students to take a moment before their discussion to jot down some ideas that they want to include in their conversation. Students also collect questions, issues, or events in their journals as they read. During discussion, a quick glance at the list may be all students need to remember what they wanted to bring up with the group.

After Discussion

Some students have difficulty coming up with something to write about in their journals. After a discussion, students have many ideas bouncing around in their heads. The arguments and wonderings are fresh and can often be captured and sorted out through writing. It may be easier to grasp one or two ideas to explore further in their written response. Journal writing can help students to analyze, synthesize, and regener-ate what they think, feel, believe, and understand as a result of a conversation with others.

As Part of Debriefing

I also use writing to help students evaluate the conversation itself. Sometimes we will debrief out loud as a whole group. At other times, I want to know more than I might get when stu-dents have to speak in public. I find that students may be more honest and open when they write about what's going well and what still needs work in their discussions. When students debrief in their journals, they answer the same two questions I use for the oral debriefing: "What is going well?" and "What do you still need to work on?"

Developing Written Response Over Time

My use of writing in literature circles has evolved in phases similar to my growth with discussions. Each represents a stage in my development as a teacher, and the successes and frustrations I encountered in each phase led me to my next steps.

Phase 1: Nondirected Response

I call Phase 1 my menu phase. When I began, each student had a spiral notebook dedicated to literature circles and wrote six journal entries per book. I made this great poster for my class called, "Journal Writing Ideas." We listed familiar forms of written response, such as a letter to a character, a letter to the author, and a Venn diagram. I modeled examples of each. Students wrote because it was assigned and rarely added insight or depth to their thoughts. They complained about not having enough to say, and their responses were brief and superficial.

I realized that the list we had generated in class was too broad for many students. Although they had experience with various ways of writing about what they read, my students weren't invested in the response. Picking their form of written response hadn't inspired the deep thinking I was hoping to evoke.

In addition, some of the forms of writing on the list provoked shallow responses. The Venn diagram, for example, inspired single-word comparisons and contrasts rather than extended analysis. Students chose Venn diagrams when they didn't want to write. Similarly, students who wrote diary entries often resorted to retelling the story. Letters to authors were usually opinions—sometimes expressed in a very critical tone, rarely giving supporting evidence and detail. I also found that strong readers could choose an appropriate response, such as a Venn diagram, at a point in the book where they really had something to compare. Less able readers, however, often chose a form of response that didn't fit the book and that didn't show much about their understanding of the text.

During this time, I happened to be taking part in a literature circle with my teaching colleagues. We deliberately tried out every component of literature circles that we required of our students. We wrote six journal entries for our adult book, and we quickly discovered that writing so often was a pain. This experience led me to rethink the purpose and frequency of written response in my classroom.

Phase 2: Directed Response

I thought that the solution to improving the quality of written response was to be more directive; hence Phase 2. Figure 5-2 shows the form I used next, asking students to do three very specific tasks. First they summarized the section or chapters of the book they just read, then they added a few questions to bring to their next discussion. Finally, they used the bottom half of the page to write a response.

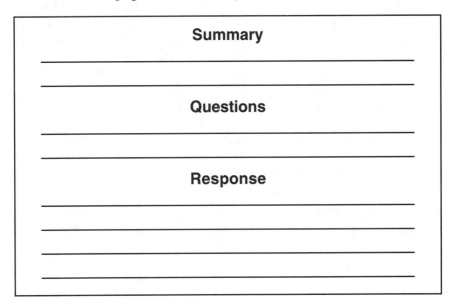

Figure 5-2: Structured Response Journals

The amount of direction I provided depended on the time of year, my students' experience with literature circles, and their writing skills. I required students to turn in two journal entries each week. At the beginning of the year, I gave students a prompt for the response section of each entry, such as "Describe the setting of this story" or "What do you think of the book so far? Why?" As students became more proficient, I offered a prompt for one entry and gave students a choice for the second response. As soon as I noticed their responses becoming longer, I dismantled the scaffolding of the form and moved to lined paper and fewer prompts for the next literature circle unit.

However, students were still not exhibiting the depth I sought. They were just filling in the blanks. I wondered, "Do I need to spend more time teaching to the form? Or do I need to change the structure?"

Phase 3: Structured but Open Response

I stepped into Phase 3 one day by accident. During the read-aloud of *Tangerine* (Bloor, 1997), I looked up and said, "Stop. What are you thinking right now?" I began recording their ideas on an overhead transparency and had a full page in no time. This showed students the range of responses people can have to the same passage. The next time I read aloud, I asked students for a quick write in their journals. Everybody wrote at least half a page. Kate later told me the following:

> I remember when I read *King of Shadows* (Cooper, 1999) and responded as a freewrite. Suddenly I had filled up a whole page without even realizing it. It wasn't my best writing, but it was my most honest feelings about the book.

I think it was that spontaneous moment to "think aloud on paper," paired with the intensity of the story, that helped me to see what was missing from the literature circle journals. Students had a lot to say—they just needed the right guidance to get it down on paper. Notice how Sarah's response to *Tangerine* is immediate and specific.

> After hearing that chapter, I think that Paul is walking into a whole other environment. He might have thought that it would be better there. I also think there is some foreshadowing when Teresa said her brother and his friends wouldn't be at soccer practice. It makes you think that they vandalized the

freak show. I feel glad for Paul right now because he
feels like he gets to start off new and is happy but I
also feel suspenseful because I don't feel it will last.
Once the boys that were suspended come back, I
don't think Paul will be happy.

There's something about being in a community of writers
that can inspire students to dig more deeply. Rather than writing at home with all the distractions that tug on adolescents,
writing together in class helps my students to think. Even students who were not strong writers seemed to focus more and
write more thoughtfully during the quick writes based on the
read-aloud book. As I read through their journal entries, I was
able to listen in on their thinking and to see clearly what they
were getting out of the book in a more immediate way. I
asked a few students to share these quick responses in order
to model various ways of responding to a text.

As a result of the quick writes, students began to write in
their journals with more depth. I experimented with specific
prompts based on focus lessons, such as "Include why you
think the author chose to tell the story from this point of
view. How would it have been different if the author had told
the story from a different character's point of view?" or "What
technique does the author use to hook the reader?" My more
reluctant writers particularly seemed to need these focused literary questions. Stronger writers leapt at the chance to be
more creative. For instance, Kate wrote, "My favorite type of
journal entry is putting myself in the main character's shoes. I
love trying to re-create the character's voice so it sounds realistic. It's a good feeling to read over what you've written and
think, 'Wow. That sounds just like that character.'"

I also found success with responses written to open-ended
prompts such as "I feel...," "I wonder...," I think... because...." However, I used one at a time, not all three at
once. Students began to let me see what they were really
thinking. My students needed a framework to start them
thinking and writing, but they didn't need me to tell them
what to write.

I want writing to flow out of students' heads, but it still has
to be channeled. As I work to inspire greater depth of response, I want students to take pride in their journals, captur-

ing in their writing the thoughtful, inspiring ideas I hear in their discussions. For that reason, I've moved to a form of written response that elicits greater depth in student writing while achieving a balance between structure and openness.

Writing Response Journals Today

Because I believe that the support of a community of writers is so important, the majority of journal writing occurs in class, not assigned as homework. Journals are primarily blank paper where students capture their thinking as they dig deeper into the books they read. The format and components vary with each unit. Journals usually include a cover and pages for gathering "Golden Lines" and interesting words. In the rest of the journal, students write a wide variety of responses, such as student-generated topics, reflections and debriefings, quick writes, "Sketch to Stretch," and the Four-Column Journal Entry.

Golden Lines

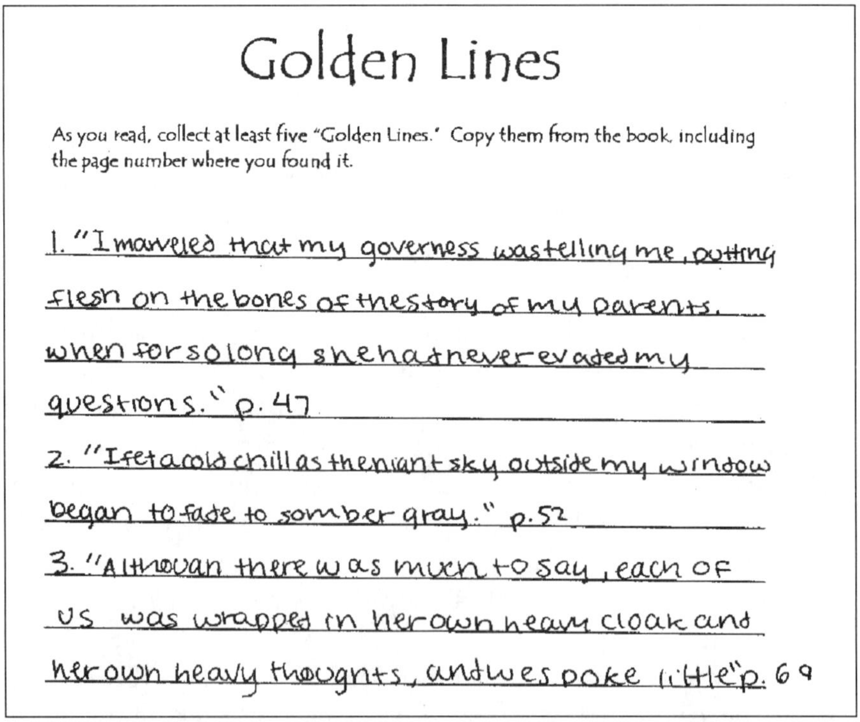

Golden Lines

As you read, collect at least five "Golden Lines." Copy them from the book, including the page number where you found it.

1. "I marveled that my governess was telling me, putting flesh on the bones of the story of my parents, when for so long she had never evaded my questions." p. 47

2. "I felt a cold chill as the night sky outside my window began to fade to somber gray." p. 52

3. "Although there was much to say, each of us was wrapped in her own heavy cloak and her own heavy thoughts, and we spoke little." p. 69

Figure 5-3: Golden Lines

On a designated page in the journal, students gather Golden Lines—quotes from the book that stand out as they read (Figure 5-3). Students use their Golden Lines as evidence or inspiration in their discussions and in written response. By listing the page numbers of the Golden Lines, students can refer back to the book during discussions.

Golden Lines provide good examples of word choice, details, and descriptive writing. This technique also helps students to analyze the author's writing style and compare styles of different writers. For example, as they compared their Golden Lines from *Jason's Gold* (1999), my students discovered that Will Hobbs uses many similes. By analyzing an author's writing at the sentence level, students can more easily grasp literary elements—such as author's craft—that seem elusive and abstract.

Interesting Words (Vocabulary)

The journals also include a page on which students collect interesting words (Figure 5-4). If I called this form "New Vocabulary," I know my students would resist. Who wants to admit they don't know hard words? Focusing on words that pique readers' interest provides a meaningful way for me to teach vocabulary and for students to show their understanding of the more challenging words they encounter. I ask students to include a definition in their own words, which also reinforces vocabulary knowledge and the use of context clues. I encourage students to compare their own definitions to the one in the dictionary to make sure that their definitions are accurate. Students often talk about these words during discussions.

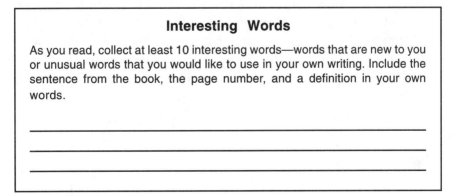

Interesting Words

As you read, collect at least 10 interesting words—words that are new to you or unusual words that you would like to use in your own writing. Include the sentence from the book, the page number, and a definition in your own words.

Figure 5-4: Interesting Words

In Figure 5-5, Laura defined several words from *Elizabeth I* (Lasky, 1999) and even glued in a picture of a "hauberk" to enrich her definition. When I read this entry, I chuckled at Laura's definition of "decrepitude."

Interesting Words

As you read, collect at least ten interesting words, words that are new to you, unusual or words that you would like to use in your own writing. Include the sentence from the book, the page number and a definition in your own words.

- Pavane p. 96 She dances a very good pavane.
  *A midieval dance.

- Syllogism p. 97 So every evening I am required to prepare for the next for the next days lesson examples of the basic forms of logical arguments: syllogisms.. *A kind of argument (ie. If all men are goats, and all goats are happy then all men are happy).

- Hauberk p.70 We got frightfully hot and finally took of the hauberks and just wore our mail vests which were much cooler. *A tunic. worn over chain mail.

  This is such a good idea! I think I'll add it to the requirements!

- Decrepitude p.119 It is after 30 that decrepitude begins to set in - unfortunately for women more quickly than men *the state of being weak or worn.

Figure 5-5: Example of Interesting Words

These vocabulary words provide another possible topic for discussion as students share the different words they have collected. I urge students to use these new words in their writing, celebrating publicly when I see evidence of this reading and writing connection. As you can see from my comment on Laura's picture of the hauberk, I often use students' spontaneous contributions to refine my requirements.

Student-Generated Topics

When students are about halfway through the book, I ask them to list possible discussion or writing topics. By this point, they are usually invested in the lives and challenges of the characters and have a lot to say. Here is the list that Cora developed for *Mary, Bloody Mary* (Meyer, 1999):

1. How dramatic it was when Anne was beheaded

2. The letter from Catherine of Aragon before her death

3. How Mary changed throughout the book

4. The author's style. Have you read other books in this time period? If so, how do they compare?

5. After rereading the prologue, do you think that Mary had good reasons to hate Anne?

After generating her list, Cora wrote the following:

> It kind of seems like Mary is actually older than she really is. If you compare her life as a 12-year-old then to now, you would see a large difference. I think that times were so different then. I wouldn't want to be a princess back then because of all the restrictions. You have to act a certain way, be a certain way. Those times kind of prevented people of their creativity. The most creative thing they are allowed is sewing. The times also kind of stole the childhood of many people.

Reflection and Debriefing

As described in chapter 4, I periodically ask for a quick written reflection about the discussion. I ask students to focus specifically on what they contributed, what went well, and what could be better. Students reflect after the first discussion, midway through the book, and then at the end of the book. These debriefings provide an ongoing record of how students' discussion and writing skills develop together.

"Sketch to Stretch"

One way to encourage students to think and talk about symbolism is to provide a blank piece of paper at the end of the journals where students can do quick sketches as they read. Students add to their sketches as they read and learn more about the book and the characters. "Sketch to Stretch"

(Harste, Short, & Burke, 1988) provides a way for students to respond to literature artistically. Students can share their evolving drawings during discussions throughout the book. In Figure 5-6, you can see how Kayla used words and symbols to convey the themes and images from *The Outsiders* (Hinton, 1967).

Figure 5-6: Sketch to Stretch

I model this technique on the overhead using the class read-aloud novel. I say, "Tell me about some colors or symbols that come to mind so far in the book" and then sketch these on a transparency.

Four-Column Journal Entry

The Four-Column Journal Entry requires more time, thought, and effort than other forms of written response. Therefore, I usually introduce it after I'm sure students can effectively express their ideas on paper. I also use it sparingly; the nature of the interaction would lose its power if it were assigned too frequently. Figure 5-7 shows the format for the Four-Column Journal Entry.

Summary	My Response	Peer Response	My Response

Figure 5-7: Four-Column Journal Entry

Students divide two pieces of lined notebook paper in half down the middle of the page. In the first column, they summarize the section that they read. In the second column, they respond to characters' actions, events in the story, and/or their overall feelings about the book so far. For instance, in her second column, Kayla reacted to *The Call of the Wild* (London, 1903) as follows:

> At first, I groaned when I heard that we would have to read *The Call of the Wild.* It was getting in the way of everything else until finally I just gave up and read it. How could something so bothersome be this good? Personally, I loved the book. When I found out it was 100 years old, I was stunned! The book is definitely going to end up on my "Books to Suggest and Spread" list. I can't wait to share it with my friends who haven't yet read it!

Students then exchange journals with assigned partners who read what has been written and add their response in the third column. The journal is returned to the original author, who completes the exchange by writing a final reflection in the fourth column.

This type of interactive dialogue journal has solved one of my most enduring challenges in inspiring students' written response: How do I get them to dig deep, to take it seriously, and to capture their thoughts on paper? Let's take a look at how this is illustrated in the exchange between two students. First, here is Kate's journal entry about *The Maze* by Will Hobbs (1999):

> My prediction for the next few chapters is that Rick will try hang gliding himself. When Lon explained to him what he was doing when attaching the harness, Rick seemed nervous, but also mildly interested. I like the way the author expressed the growing relationship between Lon and Rick. Lon is gradually gaining Rick's trust and vice-versa. It would not be realistic if the two were 'buddy-buddy' from their meeting. Using subtle hints, like Lon using Rick's nickname ('Maverick') for the condor demonstrates this.

When Taylor read Kate's response, he was impressed and wrote back:

> You did a great job! (A lot better than me). I liked the way you used eighth grade words like "mildly interested" and "vice-versa." I have a feeling that you will one day be a famous writer!

Kate replied:

> Thanks so much for your compliments, Taylor. I'm not sure if I'd like to be an author when I grow up. . . . That's a ways off. I have to survive this year first!

Students quickly discover how difficult it is to respond to someone whose written reaction is minimal or who is "faking." Here is part of an exchange between two students about *The Maze* (Hobbs, 1999):

> Some of the parts you wrote aren't true, so I'm assuming you skim read it. Like where you said Rick hops out of the car that was nice enough to pick him up. He really jumped into the back of the truck when the guy wasn't looking.

His partner confessed:

> I did skim read around 10–20 pages because it was pretty boring at one part and now I'm sorry I did because you can tell I did. I liked that you told me what part was true and I won't skim read if there's another boring part!

The Four-Column Journal Entry shows students that they have an audience in addition to me—their peers. When they reveal their thinking to someone else, they feel a greater need to have something worth saying. This form also taps into some of the most potent needs of adolescents: to have choices, to interact socially, to be heard, and to write for real purposes.

Choice. Although the summary entry is structured in format, the content of the response entry is wide open. The second column sets the tone for the conversation. If students simply revisit their summary, there isn't much for the partner to say. On the other hand, if they express their original thoughts and opinions, there's more for their partner to work with in responding.

Social Interactions. My students crave time to talk to one another. This format allows some of that interaction, albeit focused and purposeful. They get to see how someone other than the teacher responds to their thinking, and they gradually learn how to express themselves more clearly and persuasively.

Audience. By using these entries, my students quickly understand that someone will listen to what they have to say. Unlike discussions, when some students have a hard time getting their voices heard, they all know that a reader will respond to their writing.

Real Purposes. Finally, the third column for peer response stretches my students to build on the ideas of others. It puts real responsibility on both writers to be clear and accurate and honest. As they grow more comfortable with this type of writing, I see students using their writing to express what's inside their heads and hearts, and sometimes their peers take them more seriously as a result.

Covers

The final component of the response journal is the cover, which we save for "dessert" at the end of the unit. I show examples from previous years and talk about quality. This artistic project helps students to view their journals as quality products that foster a sense of pride and brings closure to the literature circle unit. I encourage students to use various art forms, including drawing, collage, and computer graphics. In Figure 5-8, you can see an example of Kasey's artistic cover for *The Maze* (Hobbs, 1999).

Figure 5-8: Journal Cover

Focus Lessons for a Written Response

Focus lessons help me to guide and refine students' expertise as writers. Here are some of the focus lessons that have helped my middle school students to grow as writers and responders:

- What to look for in Golden Lines
- Collecting interesting words

- Using peer response to help you respond more thought-fully
- Evoking response through writing
- Using journals to prepare for discussions
- Using quotes with page numbers to support opinions
- Using examples from the book to show your under-standing
- Debriefing discussions through writing
- Setting goals
- Developing your thinking through sketching
- Illustrating journal covers

Most of my focus lessons come directly from what my students and I experience as we write. Every time we hit a roadblock, there's another focus lesson. For example, many of my students made predictions in their journals. They loved speculating on the future direction of the plot or character development. However, they rarely explained why they thought a particular event might happen. I pulled a few examples from students' journals to use as a focus lesson. Together we found quotes from the book and formulated explanations that would substantiate their predictions. The more I show samples of quality journal responses, the more time and effort my students put into their work. Knowing the target helps students to understand my expectations.

Focus lessons have two main components: sharing student samples and using the overhead projector or white board to model written response.

Sharing Samples

I save samples from previous classes that illustrate various aspects of writing that I want my current students to master. As I put the sample on the overhead projector, I'll ask, "Why is this a good response?" and "What could be better?" Students often recognize more about quality response than they can deliver themselves. The concrete examples help me clarify my expectations. The following example compares the conflict in *The Outsiders* (Hinton, 1967), to *Nothing but the Truth* (Avi, 1991). I pointed out to my students how the writer compared two books and backed up her opinion:

> One thing I just noticed was how this book is like *Nothing but the Truth*. In both of these books, the author shows how a small conflict or something like that gets bigger and bigger until it gets out of hand. In *The Outsiders*, it is the Soc and Greaser conflict, and in the other book it's about the national anthem.

Modeling Written Response

Sharing my own writing on the overhead projector is more intimidating for me but often very powerful for my students. Here is a response I wrote in front of my students when we read aloud *Tangerine* (Bloor, 1997):

> I keep wondering what really happened to Paul to damage his eyesight. It obviously has something to do with his older brother since the author keeps giving us clues, such as Paul's flashbacks when his brother is chasing him with a baseball bat. I think the confidence Paul is developing at his new school as a result of making new friends and doing well on the soccer team will help him stand up to his brother's bullying. I feel anxious that something is about to explode soon. There is so much that is still unsettled and we are almost to the end of the book. There are so many loose ends that still need to be tied up. I hope this isn't one of those books where the author just leaves the resolution for the reader to figure out!

I used this example to show my students how to respond to a book at a particular point in the story. My modeling shows students how readers converse internally.

Responding to and Evaluating Student Writing

Writers need readers. One of the best ways I've found to provide responsive readers is to guide students to respond to each other's work by using the Four-Column Journal Entry. However, I also need to share my insights, guidance, and support as a teacher and adult reader and writer. I am as concerned about students keeping up with their writing as I am about their development as writers. Therefore, I give immediate feedback as they are writing journal entries. Walking around the room, I look over their shoulders, affirm their efforts, and offer support when needed. In addition to coaching students as they write, I evaluate more formally, using written comments and a 4-point scale for grading.

Written Comments

When I first started using response journals, I felt compelled to respond to each entry from each student in every class. Of course, I felt overwhelmed. Now I glance through journals periodically, particularly those of students about whom I'm concerned. Although I give informal feedback as students write, I don't respond in writing until the end of the unit. At that time, I write specific comments on Post-it® notes. Although occasionally the Post-it® notes disappear and parents may not see them, they seem more respectful than writing in the margins of the student's work.

The key to responding is to be specific. For instance, in Cora's journal, I wrote, "Excellent response. You reacted to Sarah's comments in your original entry but still continued to build your own ideas." Sometimes I will raise questions in the journals, such as "Why do you think this?" For report cards or conferences, I can synthesize each student's growth in writing by skimming over the comments I've made in the journals and noting whether or not the student took my suggestions.

Four-Point Grading Scale

Response journals comprise 25 percent of students' grade for reading. As with discussions, I use a 4-point scale to evaluate written response. I read through each student's journal at the end of a literature circle unit, then score the whole journal holistically. A 1 or 2 signifies that students are simply retelling the storyline. I'll give a 3 to students who probe a little deeper, although the journal entry may simply reiterate the points made in class. In order to get a 4, students have to back up their opinion by referring to the text or providing examples. I give 4s sparingly, only to students who "run with their own ideas" and who use writing as a way of making connections and exploring their thoughts about a book.

Sample journal entries provide models for my students. In order for students to understand my expectations, I created a bulletin board with sample written responses (Figure 5-9) that represented each level of the 4-point scale. Below each entry, I also explained possible improvements for each entry. This chart provides specific benchmarks for students as they develop their own written responses.

1	2	3	4
Roll of Thunder, Hear My Cry So far, I think the book is pretty good.	***Goodnight, Mr. Tom*** I really like this book so far. Mr. Tom seems kind of mean. I think maybe he will change. I wonder what is wrong with Willie. This book reminds me of a movie I once saw. I think it's interesting how they sent the children out of London during the war.	***Let the Circle Be Unbroken*** On page 245 when Cassie said, "Stuart had made an embarrassing mistake, and I knew that it wasn't going to be very pleasant when he realized what it was," she meant that Stuart had not realized that Suzella was mostly black, and was treating her like she was white. When he found out that he had been respectful toward a black person, he would be angry and embarrassed.	***The Invisible Thread*** I think this book is called *The Invisible Thread*, because when Yoshiko's mother left Japan to come to America she never really left Japan behind. An "invisible thread," as Yoshiko called it, was wrapped around her mother, never letting her become truly American. When Keiko and Yoshiko were born the thread was tied around them, too, because of their looks, beliefs, style of life, and heritage their mother passed on to them. Even though Yoshiko hated being Japanese and wanted to fit in with American society, she couldn't deny who she was. It was the "invisible thread" that kept her from being a true American.
• Inadequate amount of writing. • Contains no substance. • Does not demonstrate any knowledge or support an opinion about the book.	• Writing is a little brief. • Includes no examples or explanations. • This would be a very good entry if it answered questions like: Why do you like the book? Why does Mr. Tom seem so mean? What movie does this remind you of, and why?	• Adequate amount of writing to support an idea. • Includes a specific example and an interpretation of the quote. • Demonstrates an understanding of the characters.	• Thorough writing, that includes a clear, detailed explanation as support. • Demonstrates interpretation beyond the stated text. There is evidence of reading "between the lines." • Evidence of an understanding of the theme of the book.

Figure 5-9: Response Journal Rubric

Student Self-Evaluation

At the end of the year, I ask students to read through their journals from the year and reflect on what they have done well and how they could improve, as well as specific plans about how they can accomplish these goals. In June, Laura wrote the following:

> I think I am doing a great job of responding artistically to literature, as well as generating good written responses. I think I have improved in using reasons to support my statements.
>
> I would like to improve by keeping up my Golden Lines and Interesting Words and drawing more connections to other books, movies, and events. I would like to think about these things more as I read instead of after I complete the book.

My Own Goals for Written Response

I continue to read professional books, talk to colleagues, and question the best way to use written response to help my students dig deeper into the books they read. Here are two specific goals for my next steps with written response to literature.

Moving Toward Blank Paper

I believe that the most powerful form is a blank piece of paper. I'm working on weaning myself and my students from preprinted forms to the wide-open possibilities of notebook paper. For strong readers and writers, the open page is more inviting. Cora wrote as follows:

> Sometimes the responses seemed too form-fitted and I wanted to say my opinions, but with the form, it was too hard to say what I wanted to say. I like it better when I can write whatever I want and I can just let my ideas flow.

I want my students to be able to write spontaneously and learn to use writing as a way to discover what they think and feel.

Reading Like Writers, Writing Like Readers

I want to continue to push my students to read with an eye toward writing, and to write with an ear for reading. For example, my students find such intriguing quotes to talk about in their conversations. I want them to be able to use those Golden Lines as jumping-off points for their writing. My goal is for students to see writing as a way to continue the thinking that a book has sparked.

Writing helps students to look inside themselves. Most middle schoolers are reluctant to let others know how they feel. If I can create a safe environment, students can grab hold of their feelings, take them out and look them over, and share them with others—and ultimately understand themselves more deeply.

Chapter 6 ⮡

Extending Response
through the Arts

I can't express what I know about something very well on paper. It's kind of like football in my head. My brain passes information to my hand, but something intercepts it on the way.

—Student, Grade 7

For many students, art levels the playing field. Talking or writing about what they think can be hard. Spreading their thoughts out in the open for others to read and hear can be agony. The visual and performing arts sometimes help students to make themselves understood. When I give students a chance to express themselves through art, some students really blossom.

What Are Extension Projects?

Extension projects are artistic responses that extend and enhance students' enjoyment, appreciation, and understanding of literature. They give students an opportunity to revisit their books, make connections between the literature and their own lives, and gain a clear picture of how all of the books are connected by a common theme. Regie Routman (1994) describes the relationship between literature circles and extension projects as follows: "A worthwhile literature extension activity grows naturally out of the literature, encourages students to thoughtfully re-examine the text, and demonstrates something the reader has gained from the book" (p. 87). Extension projects can incorporate art, music, creative writing, technology, dance, or drama.

Purpose of Extension Projects

Extension projects keep the thinking and response alive even after students have finished a book. The goal is to lure students back into the book to cement, extend, and even reinvent what they gained from their first visit. As they plan and prepare their projects, students continue the conversations with each other. In his book on literature circles, Harvey Daniels (2002) describes this social benefit of response projects:

> At one level, this is a way for readers to pull together their own thinking about a book, to celebrate and culminate their reading. . . . The sharing . . . can also provide a nice change of pace, a coming together, an opportunity for students to discuss, perform, or connect their reading. (p. 90)

Sample Extension Projects

I've used many of the project ideas described in detail in professional books such as *Literature Circles and Response* (Hill, Johnson, & Schlick Noe, 1995) and *Getting Started With Literature Circles* (Schlick Noe & Johnson, 1999). Figure 6-1 includes some of my favorites.

Main Idea Belt: 5–6 connected paper disks representing the main events, with illustrations on one side and explanations on the other.

Collage: Symbols and pictures cut from magazines representing the characters and themes

Literary Weaving (Johnson, 1997): Adding machine tape strips filled with words and symbols, which are then woven together into a quilt

Character Bookmark: Illustration of a main character on the front with a written description on the back

Commemorative Stamp: Illustration or symbol with a Golden Line, key word, or phrase representing the theme

ABC Book: Each page contains an illustration and a sentence featuring a letter of the alphabet that describes a chapter, event, or key scene

Setting Pamphlet: Trifold pamphlet filled with illustrations and captions of key places in the book

Readers Theatre: A student-written script re-creating a major scene, then rehearsed and read aloud to the class without props or costumes

Photo Album: Illustrations of main characters, events, and settings with captions

Timeline: A series of main events, including dates and brief descriptions in chronological order

Game Board: Game created around the characters, events, or theme of the book

Poetry: All types of poetry written to capture the essence of a main character or of the story

Mural: A large painting depicting one or several important scenes and characters

Story Quilt: Several illustrated squares representing the main events or chapters of a book, decorated with symbols on the borders and including Golden Lines

Story Map: An illustrated map outlining the journey of the main character, sometimes using three dimensional objects

Debate: Two teams debate opposite sides of an issue using evidence from the book

PowerPoint: A series of slides depicting main events, story elements, or character development

Figure 6-1: Sample Extension Projects

Teaching the Process

When I first started using extension projects, I fumbled a bit. I began to realize what was wrong during a reenactment of a scene from *Roll of Thunder, Hear My Cry* (Taylor, 1976). The "skit" was actually just a pile of sixth-grade boys lying on the floor and rolling around. Lots of action; no point. I realized that a project has to have some substance. I also recognized that the audience wasn't just me as the evaluator, but also students' peers as fellow readers.

Now I begin by helping students to understand what it means to *extend* a book. The project must expand on and deepen students' experience of the book, and it must add onto what the rest of us understand as well. I emphasize this point over and over. Students need to hear it many times.

I think that it's important to provide time in class for students to work on their extension projects. As students revisit the text together, they often dig deeper, and some of the best conversations occur as they create these collaborative projects. The strategies I use to teach the process of extension projects are the following:

- Begin with a whole class project, then offer choices
- Show good examples and clarify expectations
- Explain the steps involved
- Emphasize that extension projects involve thinking
- Offer project choices

Begin with a Whole-Class Project

Early in the year, I select one project that all students complete. I find it much easier to teach the kinds of thinking involved in creating an extension project if students aren't distracted by a lot of choices. It really helps to start with something concrete. For example, when the seventh graders read *Goodnight, Mr. Tom* (Magorian, 1981), everyone contributed a square to a Story Quilt (Figure 6-2). Each student chose a chapter and created an illustration to represent the main idea and found a Golden Line that supported their illustration.

Figure 6-2: Story Quilt

Show Good Examples

I show several examples of a finished product, either student work from previous years or my own sample project. When I encounter exemplary work, I ask permission to keep the project or to make copies.

For instance, not only is Chelsea's visual collage effective (Figure 6-3), but her written reflection that follows shows how intentionally she chose symbols that represented the theme and issues in *Shabanu* (Staples, 1989).

Figure 6-3: Collage

Beauty is in the eye of the beholder. That beautiful pair of eyes gazing at you from the top of this page signifies perspective. This book was written through the eyes of a rambunctious teenager living in a world quite unlike our own.

The way Shabanu deals with her problems and perceives her feelings is represented in the diamond because its beauty shines from the center of a rock like Shabanu. She has so much beauty in her heart but she saves some of it inside where no one can reach it.

In the background is a footprint in the sand, showing not only the terrain that Shabanu lives in Pakistan, but also the footprints she has to follow. Her ancestors long ago made these prints and everyone is forced to follow.

The mouth located in the middle of the collage represents the fact that Shabanu is not afraid to speak her mind. The sparkly shirts represent the wedding of Phulan to Murad. All the relatives of the bride dressed up in beautiful mirrored skirts and shawls.

Blue flowers were placed in clumps at the top of the page because they show the four experiences that Shabanu endured and also show that there was a shadow left behind that will always be with her. The loss of Guluban, the loss of Murad, her betrothal to an older man, and her final scheme to run away are the experiences that the roses represent.

Explain the Steps

As I show sample projects, I explain each step of the process. The specific steps change with each project. I create them based on past experience and what seems to be most logical for students to understand. For example, for the Story Quilt, students first select a main idea or theme that represents the book. Students then sketch an illustration that represents that idea and choose a Golden Line to incorporate in the picture. Next, they design a border with symbols and colors that reflect the message or theme of the book. Students complete a rough draft and then a final draft. Students share their quilt

squares in the order of the chapters, and explain how their illustrations and Golden Lines represent the main idea of each
chapter. As each square is added, the quilt takes shape, cap-
turing the essence of the novel.

Every year, students' extension projects improve as they
build on each other's ideas. The Story Quilt is a good example
of how my expectations for extension projects have changed
over time. The first year, my students simply drew a picture
representing something symbolic from the book. However, I
found that students all chose the same symbols, such as
hearts or teardrops. Now I ask each person to choose a different chapter in the book and to envision a symbol that best
represents that chapter. I also ask students to include a
Golden Line and to explain on the back of the square how
the quote synthesizes some important aspect of the book.

Emphasize Thinking

I spend a great deal of time explaining the thought processes
that go into a project. It's so important to be explicit about
the purpose and criteria for each extension project. I ask students the following questions (Schlick Noe & Johnson, 1999,
pp. 93–94) before they begin to work on their projects:

- How will my project show what I have learned
  from the book?
- In what ways will my project include information
  from the book?
- When people view my project, what will they learn
  about my book?

My hope is that students not only show what they have
learned from a book, but that they teach each other about the
layers of meaning in a text.

Introduce Choices

Once students understand the purposes and processes of extension projects, I gradually introduce choices. I might offer
three choices that specifically match the themes of the books
they are reading. Because of their experience with a variety of

extension projects, eighth graders choose from a wider menu or propose their own ideas not on the list of choices. For instance, after finishing a unit on Shakespeare's time, I formed groups of four students who had each read a different novel and had them do an extension project together. Justin, Kate, Anders, and Hillary created a game called "The Shakespeare Dealer" (Figure 6-4), based on the four books in the unit on Shakespeare's time (see Figure 2-6). The trivia and chance cards created for the game integrated key ideas from all four books and demonstrated students' broad understanding of the books and time period.

Figure 6-4: Game Board

Another group decided to do a PowerPoint presentation, consisting of digital photographs they took of themselves, combined with a dramatic script. The result was similar to a movie, communicating in an entertaining fashion the important events and characters of each of the four books.

Some books naturally lend themselves to certain forms of artistic response. Therefore, when I create the list of project choices, I think about which extensions would best fit each unit. For example, the clear themes and issues in *Goodnight Mr. Tom* (Magorian, 1981) work well for a Story Quilt or an alphabet book. For *Jason's Gold* (Hobbs, 1999), story maps are a great way for students to depict the action and character development represented by Jason's journey to the Klondike gold fields. Figure 6-5 shows how Tina and Cora created a visual representation of the setting of the book, including a map that traces Jason's journey, a newspaper article, and photographs from the time period.

Figure 6-5: Story Map

Authors' Web sites can be great resources for project ideas that are meaningfully tied to particular books. For example, Will Hobbs's Web site (www.willhobbsauthor.com) provided helpful ideas that I added to my menu for 5 response projects based on *Jason's Gold* (Figure 6-6). On the same Web site, I also discovered several related nonfiction books that filled in the context of the Gold Rush era. For instance, *Yukon Gold: The Story of the Klondike Gold Rush* (Jones, 1999) has photographs of the newspaper clippings, the people, and the places in the Yukon that students read about in *Jason's Gold*. Students not only extended what they knew about *Jason's Gold*, but also broadened their reading about this historical event and time period.

One thing I've discovered is that students are willing to invest more time and energy on extension projects for books they enjoy reading. For instance, Cora told me that she didn't like doing projects when she didn't care for the book. On the other hand, she said, "If I liked the book, making an extension project was like dessert after a good dinner. It was kind of like reading the book again."

1. **PEN PALS:** Jason admired Jack London and was grateful for his help. After Jack London returned back home, imagine that Jason kept in touch by writing letters. He would want to tell Jack not only about events up in Dawson and the race to Nome, but about his feelings about being up North, and about making a life for himself in this wild country. You might want to do this with a partner, one of you writing as Jason to Jack and the other person taking the role of Jack London as he responds to Jason's letters. (2 people)

2. **TRAVELING THE YUKON:** Read the book *Yukon River* (Lourie, 2000). It is filled with photos and firsthand accounts of the author's modern-day canoe journey down the Yukon River. Share the photos and adventures of Peter Lourie with the class while comparing and contrasting his trip with Jason's voyage. (1 or 2 people).

3. **YOU DON'T KNOW JACK:** Read *Jack London: A Biography* by Daniel Dyer (1997). Share what you have learned about this author with the class. Be sure to compare what Dyer has to say with Will Hobbs's portrayal of Jack London. Does Will Hobbs portray Jack London realistically in *Jason's Gold*? Were Jack London's experiences similar to Jason's? (1 person)

4. **CREMATING SAM MCGEE:** Jamie's father, Homer Dunavant, is loosely based on the famous poet, Robert W. Service, whose poetry captured the excitement and hardship of the Yukon Gold Rush. One of his most famous poems is "The Cremation of Sam McGee." Memorize the poem and put together a dramatic interpretation to present to the class. (1–5 people)

5. **MAPPING JASON'S JOURNEY:** Create a story map that illustrates Jason's journey from the beginning of the book to the end. Be sure to highlight all the important stops along the way. Include an explanation of the significance of each part of the journey. (1–3 people)

Figure 6-6: Extension Project Choices for *Jason's Gold*

Exploring Literary Elements Through Projects

Other projects are helpful for focusing on specific literary elements. Keith explored central events in *Maniac Magee* (Spinelli, 1990) by creating a Main Idea Belt, illustrating key ideas on one side of each circle and explaining their importance on the back (Figure 6-7).

Figure 6-7: Main Idea Belt

Sam drew a picture of Little Man from *Roll of Thunder, Hear My Cry* (Taylor, 1976) on the back of his Character Bookmark (Figure 6-8) and described the character's importance, personality traits, and his own reactions.

Little Man is the prototype of everyone's little brother. He is the type who drives you crazy by how slowly he walks to school. Little man is important because he suffers through every thing the logans do there fore the reader learns alot through his conversations. I think little man will do some thing big later in the story. Little man always helps to carry out staceys plans. For example when he dug the ditch to get the bus stuck. I think little man would be a good friend because he is kind (unless you are unkind to him). For example, when the teacher was mean to him he was mean back but before the teacher was mean little man was nice. I don't think it would be good to throw mud at him because of his meticulousness about clothes. I think little man is a very likeable guy. He makes me laugh. One of little man's funniest personality traits is that he is so meticulous about his clothes. He is generally a very caring gentle man but can be mean if provoked. For instance when T.J. was being mean to stacey little man made sure T.J. did not get to ride in uncle Hammers car. Little man really stands up for what he believes in and can be very stubborn. He is curious and doesnt really understand why the white people have everything. I imagina a small african american kid name little man wearing overalls and a dark blue shirt with his brow skin and his hair, matted to dirt caked from the mississippi road but still curious to what might happen.

BY: Sam Kennedy

Figure 6-8: Character Bookmark

A Setting Pamphlet (Figure 6-9), such as the one Hanley created about *Homecoming* (Voigt, 1981) encourages students to examine the importance and role of the setting in a story.

Figure 6-9: Setting Pamphlet

Setting a Timeline for Extension Projects

Because students do a tremendous amount of discussing and writing as they read a novel, I've found that they only need about 1 week to complete an extension project. When I've given students more time, I haven't seen any increase in quality. In fact, most of my students don't get serious about their project until the deadline bears down upon them. I generally explain the project on a Monday, structuring time during our 90-minute language arts block that day, and again on Wednesday. Although some students can work on their extension projects at home, I always plan in-class time to help groups work together and to provide extra support for students who need guidance. The projects are shared in class on the following Monday.

Focus Lessons for Extension Projects

Most of my focus lessons are linked to specific response projects, the art medium used, or the form of dramatic response. Sample focus lessons include the following:

- Considering your audience
- Communicating theme and ideas through the arts
- Using color and white space effectively
- Designing a border
- Creating a PowerPoint presentation
- Representing ideas symbolically
- Sharing your presentation (speaking skills)
- Extending books through drama
- Writing and performing a Readers Theatre script

Evaluating Extension Projects

As I develop my process for evaluating extension projects, I keep this thought in mind: I want my students to internalize the criteria for quality work as they head into high school, where less scaffolding may be provided.

Extension projects are worth 25 percent of the reading grade. I use the same 4-point scale to evaluate extension projects as I do for discussions (chapter 4) and written response (chapter 5). Students evaluate their own extension projects after their presentation by using a fairly open-ended form. Figure 6-10, shows Kate's evaluation of the game board her group created for the unit on Shakespeare's time. She explains how the project reflected what she learned from the book, along with a sentence about what she felt went well and what she would do differently next time. She also gives herself a grade based on a 4-point scale using the Extension Project Evaluation form.

As I watch the students present their projects, I record Two Stars and a Wish (Hill, Schlick Noe, & Johnson, 2001, p. 79), in which I note two things they did well and one area that needs improvement. I also give students a holistic score of 4, 3, 2, or 1. If there is a discrepancy between the student's self-score and my score, I meet with the student for an individual

Name **Kate Haller**   Date **12/10/01**

Extension Project

I/we chose to **make a game called "The Shakespeare Dealer."**

My/our project will demonstrate what we learned about the book by **the Trivia cards, which ask questions about the books, and by including places and characters for the spaces. The title shows that the books all have something to do with Shakespeare**

④   3   2   1
exceeds   meets   approaches   does not meet
expectations   expectations   expectations   expectations

I would give my/our project a **4** because **the board looks nice, and we spent effort thinking of interesting trivia questions. We could have made the game exactly like Monopoly, but changed the rules to relate to our themes.**

One thing I am proud of is **our presentation because we made up a funny commercial to explain the game and everyone participated.**

One thing I would do differently next time is **use materials other than glitter glue that dry quickly, and use class time wisely by getting everyone involved helping make the game.**

Figure 6-10: Extension Project Evaluation

conference. Whenever possible, I take photos of students' response projects, which I then attach to the form. The photograph serves as a record of the project and can also be included in student portfolios. These forms and photographs can then be shared at student-led conferences. Parents enjoy seeing these, as they seldom observe group projects or dramatic presentations. Figure 6-11 shows my holistic score and my "Two Stars and a Wish" for the mural of *The Maze* (Hobbs, 1999) created by Lauren, Sarah, and Kate.

TWO STARS AND A WISH

☆ The change in Rick from the beginning to the end (bars to wings) is so evident!

☆ Your choices — colors, the river, the "time line" format — all contribute to retelling the story so well.

WISH I'd love to see more variety in materials to add texture & 3-D effect — Maybe real feathers for the wings?

I give your project a __4__.

Figure 6-11: Two Stars and a Wish

I know I'm making progress helping my students to understand what extension projects can do when they ask, "Can we combine these two?" or "We'd like to do this project, but we'd like to do it this way." As students come up with original ideas, when they see how others make sense of and revisit books through art (and sometimes drama and music), and when they negotiate as they're working together, I know that they're internalizing the *extend* in *extension*. This doesn't happen by itself, however. When I became clear about the purpose of extension projects and how they could deepen response, I was better able to articulate my expectations and convey them to my students.

The question "Why offer art as a form of response?" boils down to this. When you take all the components of literature circles, you see that some kids process their thinking best as readers, some as writers. That's how they figure out what they know. Other kids are talkers, and many are artists. By offering all of these options, you've given everybody a way to shine.

Final
Thoughts

As we write these last words, the end of the school year is in sight. The final extension projects from Janine's sixth-, seventh-, and eighth-grade classes still hang on the walls of her classroom and bulletin boards in the hallway. The eighth graders have already turned their thoughts toward high school. Gangly knots of newcomers poke their heads in the door to see where they'll be next year for language arts. As Janine starts packing up her room, she gathers a few professional books and journals to read over the summer, as well as a stack of new young adult novels. Here are our final thoughts as the school year ends.

More than anything else, middle school students want to find out who they are and where they fit in. Underneath an energetic exterior, many young people wonder if they'll measure up, if their dreams can be met, and if they can make a difference. Because middle school is the setting in which they spend a significant part of their day, Janine wants her classroom to be a place where students feel productive and valued. She seeks to create an environment in which students can make sense of the world and try to find their place within it. She has discovered that literature and response provide a perfect vehicle for this important search. In literature circles, she watches as her students wrestle with questions they don't easily express out loud but which she knows are bubbling just below the surface. Books give voice to those questions and show how people face challenges. As students respond through discussions, writing, and the arts, they have a chance to express their ideas, questions, and hopes.

We hope your visit to Janine's classroom validated some of the things you already do in your teaching and generated some new ideas for literature circles. We'd like to continue the conversation about using literature circles in middle school through the Literature Circles Resource Center Web site mentioned in chapter 3 (http://fac-staff.seattleu.edu/kschlnoe/LitCircles). Send us feedback, questions, forms, new book titles, and stories of your own. Enjoy the journey!

Appendix A

State Standards
and Literature Circles

Communication

Literature Circle Focus Lessons	Washington State Essential Academic Learning Requirements
• Listening actively	**C 1.1** Focus attention
• Note questions on bookmarks • Ask questions during discussions	**C 1.3** Check for understanding by asking questions and paraphrasing • Ask questions to clarify content and meaning, to verify judgments and inferences
• State an opinion	**C 2.1** Communicate clearly to a range of audiences for different purposes
• Build on others' comments • Back up ideas with examples	**C 2.2** Develop content and ideas
• Share response projects with good speaking skills	**C 2.1–2.5** Communicate ideas clearly and effectively to a range of audiences and purposes; develop content and ideas; use effective delivery, language, style, action, sound, and/or images to support presentations
• Start the conversation • Pull in reluctant participants • Mediate conflicts • Rescue a flagging conversation	**C 3.1, 3.2, 3.3** Use language to interact effectively and responsibly with others; work cooperatively in a group; seek agreement and solutions through discussion
• Evaluate participation in discussions, journal entries, and presentations	**C 4.1** Analyze and evaluate the effectiveness of communication • Establish and apply criteria for evaluation of one's own and others' presentations and discussions
• Link extension projects back to the book	**R 2.3** Think critically—apply information gained from reading to give a response or express insight
• Choose and share books	**R 4.3** Develop interests and share reading experiences

Reading

Literature Circle Focus Lessons	Washington State Essential Academic Learning Requirements
• Find evidence to support a point • Ask yourself (or the text) questions • Decipher unknown words	**R 1.1** Use word recognition and word meaning skills to read and comprehend text • Use a variety of strategies to comprehend words and ideas • Analyze text for a specific purpose
• Expand vocabulary	**R 1.2** Building vocabulary through reading
• Understand how authors use plot, character, setting, tone	**R 1.4** Understand elements of literature • Identify and analyze literary devices and elements
• Draw inferences about characters' actions • Use background knowledge to understand events or characters • Make connections to your life, other books, and other authors	**R 2.1** Comprehend important ideas and details • Make, confirm, or revise inferences and predictions based on text • Link characters, events, and information to prior knowledge, previous experiences, and current issues to increase understanding
• Compare characters, events, and themes across texts • Make connections between other books and your own life	**R 2.2** Expand comprehension by analyzing, interpreting, and synthesizing information and ideas • Compare, contrast, and make connections within and among texts
• Analyze and evaluate authors' craft • Support ideas with information from the book, your own life, or other books	**R 2.3** Think critically and analyze authors' use of language, style, purpose, and perspective • Apply information gained from reading to give a response or express insight • Make generalizations beyond the text to other texts, ideas, or situations

Writing

Literature Circle Focus Lessons	Washington State Essential Academic Learning Requirements

• Choose a topic or focus for journal entries
• Support ideas with information from the book, your own life, or other books
• Elaborate by using details
• Incorporate ideas from Post-it® notes into a written response
• Incorporate ideas raised during discussion into written response
	W 1.1 Develop concept and design
	  • Choose own topic
	  • Demonstrate elaboration through examples, details, facts, and/or reasons, etc.

• Use figurative, descriptive language	**W 1.2** Use style appropriate to the audience and purpose • Use figurative language and imagery
• Write a dialogue journal with a peer • Write to reflect on characters, events, and themes	**W 2.1** Write for different audiences, including self, teacher, or other personally known audience **W 2.2** Write for different purposes, including to express ideas and to reflect upon own experiences
• Write a response from a character's point of view	**W 2.3** Write in a variety of forms • Vary form, detail, and structure

• Develop criteria for effective writing
• Self-evaluate written response
• Set goals for written response
	W 4.1 Assess own strengths and needs for improvement
	  • Establish and apply own criteria to improve writing
	  • Articulate the qualities of effective writing

Appendix B

Additional
Literature Circle Books

Challenges in Other Times or Places

Angel on the Square by Gloria Whelan
The Breadwinner by Deborah Ellis
Burning Issy by Melvin Burgess
Call Me Ruth by Marilyn Sachs
Catherine, Called Birdy by Karen Cushman
The Cure by Sonia Levitin
Fever 1793 by Laurie Halse Anderson
Go and Come Back by Joan Abelove
Habibi by Naomi Shihab Nye
Lyddie by Katherine Paterson
Matilda Bone by Karen Cushman
The Midwife's Apprentice by Karen Cushman
Numbering All the Bones by Ann Rinaldi
Out of the Dust by Karen Hesse

Radical Red by James Duffy

Red Scarf Girl: A Memoir of the Cultural Revolution by Ji-Li Jiang

Stones in Water by Donna Jo Napoli

The Storyteller's Beads by Jane Kurtz

Torn Thread by Anne Asaacs

The Wall by Elizabeth Lutzeier

When My Name Was Keoko by Linda Sue Park

Confronting Prejudice

Breakaway by Paul Yee

Breaking Through by Francisco Jiménez

The Bus People by Rachel Anderson

The Cay by Theodore Taylor

The Circuit by Francisco Jiménez

Dangerous Skies by Suzanne Fisher Staples

Darby by Jonathon Scott Fuqua

Dogland by Will Shetterly

The Gold Cadillac by Mildred Taylor

Habibi by Naomi Shihab Nye

The Land by Mildred Taylor

Let the Circle be Unbroken by Mildred Taylor

Music From a Place Called Half Moon by Jean Oughton

Numbering All the Bones by Ann Rinaldi

Risk 'n Roses by Jan Slepian

Roll of Thunder, Hear My Cry by Mildred Taylor

The Skin I'm In by Sharon Flake

Spite Fences by Trudy Krisher

The Star Fisher by Laurence Yep

The Storyteller's Beads by Jane Kurtz

Under the Blood Red Sun by Graham Salisbury

Walking to the Bus-Rider Blues by Harriet Gillem Robinet

The Watsons Go to Birmingham, 1963 by Christopher Paul Curtis

Whale Talk by Chris Crutcher

When My Name Was Keoko by Linda Sue Park

Who Will Tell My Brother? By Marlene Carvell

Witness by Karen Hesse

A Woman of Her Tribe by Margaret Robinson

Coming of Age

Born in Sin by Evelyn Coleman

Flipped by Wendelin Van Draanen

From One Experience to Another, edited by M. Jerry and Helen Weiss

Hanging on to Max by Margaret Bechard

Hope Was Here by Jane Bauer

Kissing Tennessee by Kathi Appelt

Make Lemonade and *True Believer* by Virginia Euwer Wolff

Rules of the Road by Jane Bauer

Stand Tall by Joan Bauer

Stargirl by Jerry Spinelli

The True Colors of Caitlynne Jackson by Carol Lynch Williams

Whale Talk by Chris Crutcher

When I Was Your Age: Original Stories About Growing Up, edited by Amy Ehrlich

The Wish by Gail Carson Levine

Facing Challenges

Cages by Peg Kehret

Chive by Shelley A. Barre

The Color of Absence: 12 Stories About Loss and Hope, edited by James Howe

Durable Goods by Elizabeth Berg

Earthshine by Theresa Nelson

A Face First by Priscilla Cummings

A Face in Every Window by Han Nolan

Falling From Fire by Teena Booth

Give a Boy a Gun by Todd Strasser

Hanging on to Max by Margaret Bechard

Heart of a Chief by Joseph Bruchac

Just Juice by Karen Hesse

Learning to Swim: A Memoir by Ann Turner

The Maestro by Tim Wynne-Jones

Mama, Let's Dance by Patricia Hermes

Memoirs of a Bookbat by Kathryn Lasky

Memories of Summer by Ruth White

Mick Harte Was Here by Barbara Park

Midget by Tim Bowler
Moving Mama to Town by Ronder Thomas Young
Out of the Dust by Karen Hesse
Peeling the Onion by Wendy Orr
Petey by Ben Mikaelsen
Pictures of Hollis Woods by Patricia Reilly Gifff
Racing the Past by Sis Deans
Radiance Descending by Paula Fox
Raising the Shade by Doug Wilhelm
Saying It Out Loud by Joan Abelove
Say Yes by Audrey Couloumbis
Scorpions by Walter Dean Myers
Silent to the Bone by E. L. Konigsburg
Shattering Glass by Gail Giles
Spellbound by Janet McDonald
Stuck in Neutral by Terry Trueman
A Week in the Woods by Andrew Clements
What Jamie Saw by Carolyn Coman
Who Will Tell My Brother? by Marlene Carvell

Family Issues

Alida's Song by Gary Paulsen
All the Way Home by Patricia Reilly Giff
Autumn Street by Lois Lowry
The Barn by Avi
Belle Prater's Boy by Ruth White
Belle Teal by Ann M. Martin
Breaking Through by Francisco Jiménez
Chasing Redbird by Sharon Creech
The Circuit by Francisco Jiménez
Cousins by Virginia Hamilton
Dicey's Song by Cynthia Voigt
Don't You Dare Read This, Mrs. Dunphrey by Margaret
     Peterson Haddix
A Door Near Here by Heather Quarles
A Face in Every Window by Han Nolan
A Family Apart by Joan Lowry Nixon
The Falcon's Wing by Lisa Dawna Buchanan
Falling From Fire by Teena Booth

Foster's War by Carolyn Reeder
Getting Near to Baby by Audrey Couloumbis
The Graduation of Jake Moon by Barbara Park
Hanging on to Max by Margaret Bechard
Hannah in Between by Colby Rodowsky
Heaven by Angela Johnson
Ironman by Chris Crutcher
The Janitor's Boy by Andrew Clements
Journey by Patricia MacLachlan
Keeping the Moon by Sarah Dessen
Kinship by Tracy Krisher
Love, Ruby Lavender by Deborah Wiles
Memories of Summer by Ruth White
My Louisiana Sky by Kimberly Willis Holt
Our Only May Amelia by Jennifer Holm
Pictures of Hollis Woods by Patricia Reilly Gifff
Plain City by Virginia Hamilton
Racing the Past by Sis Deans
The Rain Catchers by Jean Thesman
Raising the Shade by Doug Wilhelm
Ruby Holler by Sharon Creech
Say Yes by Audrey Couloumbis
Strawberry Hill by A. LaFaye
Toning the Sweep by Angela Johnson
Tribute to Another Dead Rock Star by Randy Powell
The Year of the Sawdust Man by A. LaFaye
Zazoo by Richard Mosher

Finding a Place to Belong

Anna Casey's Place in the World by Adrian Fogelin
Asphalt Angels by Ineke Holtwijz
Boston Jane: An Adventure by Jennifer Holm
Bud, Not Buddy by Christopher Paul Curtis
Chive by Shelley A. Barre
Dave at Night by Gail Carson Levine
Everything on a Waffle by Polly Horvath
A Face in Every Window by Han Nolan
A Family Apart by Joan Lowry Nixon
Family Pose by Dean Hughes

Ghost Boy by Iain Lawrence
The Great Gilly Hopkins by Katherine Paterson
Home, edited by Michael Rosen
Homecoming by Cynthia Voigt
Jip: His Story by Katherine Paterson
The King of Dragons by Susan Cooper
The Likes of Me by Randall Beth Platt
Lucy the Giant by Sherri Smith
Moonpie and Ivy by Barbara O'Connor
Nissa's Place by A. LaFaye
Pictures of Hollis Woods by Patricia Reilly Gifff
The Pinballs by Betsy Byars
Say Yes by Audrey Couloumbis
Shizuko's Daughter by Kyoko Mori
A Week in the Woods by Andrew Clements

Friendship: Reaching Out

All Alone in the Universe by Lynne Rae Perkins
Anna Casey's Place in the World by Adrian Foglin
Bronx Masquerade by Nikki Grimes
Crash by Jerry Spinelli
The Empress of Elsewhere by Theresa Nelson
Flying Solo by Ralph Fletcher
Freak the Mighty and *Max the Mighty* by Rodman Philbrick
Hanging on to Max by Margaret Bechard
Harris and Me by Gary Paulsen
Holes by Louis Sachar
Joyride by Gretchen Olson
Letters From Inside by John Marsden
Lily's Crossing by Patricia Reilly Giff
Miracle's Boys by Jacqueline Woodson
No More Dead Dogs by Gordon Korman
Pictures of Hollis Woods by Patricia Reilly Giff
Staying Fat for Sarah Byrnes by Chris Crutcher
The View From Saturday by E. L. Konigsburg

Imagining A Different World: What If . . .?

Among the Hidden by Margaret Peterson Haddix
(and sequels)

The Ear, the Eye, and the Arm by Nancy Farmer
The Exchange Student by Kate Gilmore
Gathering Blue by Lois Lowry
The Giver by Lois Lowry
The Golden Compass by Philip Pullman (and sequels)
The House of the Scorpion by Nancy Farmer
The Last Book In the Universe by Rodman Philbrick
The Oasis by Sue Pace
Phoenix Rising by Karen Hesse
Running Out of Time by Margaret Peterson Haddix
Second Sight: Stories for the New Millennium by Avi et al.
Star Split by Kathryn Lasky
Things Not Seen by Andrew Clements
Tomorrowland: Stories About the Future, edited by Michael
    Cart
Tomorrow When the War Began by John Marsden
    (and sequels)
Turnabout by Margaret Peterson Haddix
A Wrinkle in Time by Madeleine L'Engle
Z for Zachariah by Robert C. O'Brien

Journeys

All the Way Home by Patricia Reilly Giff
Being With Henry by Martha Brooks
Breaking Through by Francisco Jiménez
Bud, Not Buddy by Christopher Paul Curtis
Chasing Redbird by Sharon Creech
The Circuit by Francisco Jiménez
Esperanza Rising by Pam Muñoz Ryan
The Golden Compass by Philip Pullman
Homecoming by Cynthia Voigt
Hope Was Here by Jane Bauer
The Likes of Me by Randall Beth Platt
Lucy the Giant by Sherri Smith
A Long Way From Chicago and *A Year Down Yonder* by
    Richard Peck
Missing May by Cynthia Rylant
Pictures of Hollis Woods by Patricia Reilly Gifff
Rules of the Road by Jane Bauer

Step Lightly: Poems for the Journey, edited by Nancy Willard
Stowaway by Karen Hesse
Takeoffs and Landings by Margaret Peterson Haddix
Thunder Cave by Roland Smith
Walk Two Moons by Sharon Creech
The Wanderer by Sharon Creech
The Watsons Go to Birmingham, 1963 by Christopher Paul Curtis
Whirligig by Paul Fleischman
The Wreckers by Ian Lawrence

Multiple Perspectives

The Brimstone Journals by Ron Koertge
Bronx Masquerade by Nikki Grimes
Bull Run by Paul Fleischman
The Dragon's Son by Sarah L. Thomson
Flipped by Wendelin Van Draanen
The Girls by Amy Goldman Koss
Give a Boy a Gun by Todd Strasser
Kissing Tennessee and Other Stories From the Stardust Dance by Kathi Appelt
Nothing But the Truth by Avi
Seek by Paul Fleischman
Shattering Glass by Gail Giles
Two Suns in the Sky by Miriam Bat-Ami
The View From Saturday by E. L. Konigsburg
Waiting for Odysseus by Clemence McLaren
Witness by Karen Hesse

Poetry

19 Varieties of Gazelle: Poems of the Middle East by Naomi Shihab Nye
Been to Yesterday: Poems of a Life by Lee Bennett Hopkins
Behind the Wheel: Poems About Driving by Janet Wong
Bronx Masquerade by Nikki Grimes
Buried Alive: The Elements of Love by Ralph Fletcher
The Dream Keeper and Other Poems by Langston Hughes
Extra Innings: Baseball Poems, edited by Lee Bennett Hopkins

The Flag of Childhood: Poems From the Middle East, edited
by Naomi Shihab Nye

I Am Wings: Poems About Love by Ralph Fletcher

I Feel a Little Jumpy Around You, edited by Naomi Shihab
Nye and Paul Janeczko

Learning to Swim: A Memoir by Ann Turner

Love That Dog by Sharon Creech

Neighborhood Odes by Gary Soto

Ordinary Things: Poems From a Walk in Early Spring by
Ralph Fletcher

The Place My Words are Looking For, edited by Paul
Janeczko

Rising Voices: Writings of Young Native Americans edited by
Arlene Hirschfelder and Beverly Singer

*Seeing the Blue Between: Advice and Inspiration for Young
Poets*, edited by Paul Janeczko

*Shimmy, Shimmy, Shimmy Like My Sister Kate: Looking at
Harlem Through Renaissance Poems*, edited by Nikki
Grimes

Soul Looks Back in Wonder, edited by Tom Feelings

Sports Pages by Arnold Adoff

Step Lightly: Poems for the Journey, edited by Nancy Willard

Street Music: City Poems by Arnold Adoff

A Suitcase of Seaweed and Other Poems by Janet Wong

What My Mother Doesn't Know by Sonya Sones

Respecting Differences

Crazy Lady! by Jane Leslie Conly

A Face in Every Window by Han Nolan

Flip-Flop Girl by Katherine Paterson

Freak the Mighty and *Max the Mighty* by Rodman Philbrick

Ghost Boy by Iain Lawrence

The Girls by Amy Goldman Koss

The Likes of Me by Randall Beth Platt

Loser by Jerry Spinelli

Joey Pigza Loses Control by Jack Gantos

Joey Pigza Swallowed the Key by Jack Gantos

The Misfits by James Howe

Petey by Ben Mikaelsen

Probably Still Nick Swanson by Virginia Euwer Wolff
Shattering Glass by Gail Giles
The Skin I'm In by Sharon Flake
Stand Tall by Joan Bauer
Stargirl by Jerry Spinelli
Tangerine by Edward Bloor
Who Will Tell My Brother? by Marlene Carvell
Wringer by Jerry Spinelli

Small Glimpses: Short Stories

145th Street: Short Stories by Walter Dean Myers
Athletic Shorts by Chris Crutcher
Birthday Surprises: Ten Great Stories to Unwrap, edited by
Johanna Hurwitz
The Color of Absence: 12 Stories About Loss and Hope, edited
by James Howe
From One Experience to Another, edited by M. Jerry and
Helen Weiss
A Glory of Unicorns, edited by Bruce Coville
Half-Human, edited by Bruce Coville
*Kissing Tennessee and Other Short Stories From the Stardust
Dance* by Kathi Appelt
A Knot in the Grain and Other Stories by Robin McKinley
The Lion Tamer's Daughter and Other Stories by Peter
Dickinson
Odder Than Ever by Bruce Coville
On the Fringe, edited by Donald Gallo
Second Sight: Stories for the New Millennium by Avi et al.
Somehow Tenderness Survives: Stories of Southern Africa by
Hazel Rochman
Stay True: Short Stories for Strong Girls, compiled by
Marilyn Singer
Twelve Shots: Outstanding Short Stories About Guns by
Harry Mazer
Tomorrowland: Stories About the Future, edited by
Michael Cart
Water: Tales of Elemental Spirits by Robin McKinley and
Peter Dickinson

When I Was Your Age: Original Stories About Growing Up,
   edited by Amy Ehrlich

Sports and Physical Challenges

Athletic Shorts by Chris Crutcher
Baseball in April and Other Stories by Gary Soto
Bat 6 by Virginia Euwer Wolff
Born in Sin by Evelyn Coleman
Downriver by Will Hobbs
Crash by Jerry Spinelli
Extra Innings: Baseball Poems, edited by Lee Bennett
   Hopkins
Far North by Will Hobbs
The Final Game by William Roy Brownridge
Guts by Gary Paulsen
Heart of a Champion by Carl Deuker
Hoops by Walter Dean Myers
Ironman by Chris Crutcher
Slot Machine by Chris Lynch
Sports Pages by Arnold Adoff
Staying Fat for Sarah Byrnes by Chris Crutcher
Tangerine by Edward Bloor
Whale Talk by Chris Crutcher

Standing Up for Your Beliefs

Cheating Lessons by Nan Willard Cappo
Dovey Coe by Frances O'Roark Dowell
Drummers of Jericho by Carolyn Meyer
The Eagle's Shadow by Nora Martin
The Landry News by Andrew Clements
The Last Safe Place on Earth by Richard Peck
The Misfits by James Howe
Nothing But the Truth by Avi
Shattering Glass by Gail Giles
Slot Machine by Chris Lynch
Standing Up to Mr. 0. by Claudia Mills
Tangerine by Edward Bloor

Walker's Crossing by Phyllis Reynolds Naylor
Whale Talk by Chris Crutcher
Who Will Tell My Brother? by Marlene Carvell

References

Professional Books and Articles

Allen, Janet. (2000). *Yellow brick roads: Shared and guided paths to independent reading 4-12*. York, ME: Stenhouse.

Allen, Janet, & Gonzalez, Kyle. (1998). *There's room for me here: Literacy workshop in the middle school*. York, ME: Stenhouse.

Atwell, Nancie. (1998). *In the middle: New understandings about writing, reading, and learning*. (2nd ed.). Portsmouth, NH: Heinemann.

Barbieri, Maureen. (1995). *Sounds from the heart: Learning to listen to girls*. Portsmouth, NH: Heinemann.

Benson, Laura. (2002). "Strategy collections for growing readers & writers . . . and their growing teachers." *The Colorado communicator*, 25 (2), 24-38.

Benson, Laura. (2000). "The long and short of it: Short and spirited texts." *The Colorado communicator*, 25 (3), 34-50.

Brozo, William G. (2002). *To be a boy, to be a reader: Engaging teen and preteen boys in active literacy*. Newark, DE: International Reading Association.

Chevalier, Tracy. (2001). *The girl with the pearl earring*. New York: Penguin Putnam.

Combs, Martha. (1997). *Developing competent readers and writers in the middle grades*. Upper Saddle River, NJ: Merrill.

Daniels, Harvey. (1994). *Literature circles: Voice and choice in the student-centered classroom.* York, ME: Stenhouse.

Daniels, Harvey. (2002). *Literature circles: Voice and choice in book clubs and reading groups.* York, ME: Stenhouse.

Fletcher, Ralph & Portalupi, JoAnn. (2001). *Writing workshop: The essential guide.* Portsmouth, NH: Heinemann.

Harris, Violet J. (1997). *Using multiethnic literature in the K-8 classroom.* Norwood, MA: Christopher-Gordon.

Harste, Jerome, Short, Kathy, & Burke, Carolyn. (1988). *Creating classrooms for authors: The reading-writing connection.* Portsmouth, NH: Heinemann.

Harvey, Stephanie, & Goudvis, Anne. (2000). *Strategies that work: Teaching comprehension to enhance understanding.* York, ME: Stenhouse.

Hill, Bonnie Campbell, Johnson, Nancy J., & Schlick Noe, Katherine L. (Eds.). (1995). *Literature circles and response.* Norwood, MA: Christopher-Gordon.

Hill, Bonnie Campbell, Schlick Noe, Katherine L. & Johnson, Nancy J. (2001). *Literature circles resource guide.* Norwood, MA: Christopher-Gordon.

Hill, Bonnie Campbell, Ruptic, Cynthia, & Norwick, Lisa. (1998). *Classroom based assessment.* Norwood, MA: Christopher-Gordon.

Johnson, Nancy J. (September 1997). "Literary weavings: Extending response through the arts. *Voices from the middle* 4 (3), 36-39.

Moore, David M., Alvermann, Donna E., & Hinchman, Kathleen A. (Eds.). (2000). *Struggling adolescent readers: A collection of teaching strategies.* Newark, DE: International Reading Association.

Morretta, Teresa & Ambrosini, Michelle. (2000). *Practical approaches for teaching reading and writing in middle school.* Newark, DE: International Reading Association.

Paulsen, Gary. (1993). *Trumpet video visits Gary Paulsen*. New York: The Trumpet Club.

Power, Brenda Miller. (1996). *Taking note: Improving your observational notetaking*. York, ME: Stenhouse.

Raphael, Taffy, Kehus, Marcella, & Damphousse, Karen. (2001). *Book club for middle school*. Lawrence, MA: Small Planet Communications.

Rief, Linda. (1992). *Seeking diversity: Language arts with adolescents*. Portsmouth, NH: Heinemann.

Rief, Linda. (1999). *Vision and voice: Extending the literacy spectrum*. Portsmouth, NH: Heinemann.

Robb, Laura. (2000). *Teaching reading in middle school: A strategic approach to teaching reading that improves comprehension and thinking*. New York: Scholastic.

Routman, Regie. (1994). *Invitations: Changing as teachers and learners K-12*. Portsmouth, NH: Heinemann.

Rycik, James A. & Irwin, Judith. (Eds.). (2001). *What adolescents deserve: A commitment to students' literacy learning*. Newark, DE: International Reading Association.

Samway, Katharine Davies, & Whang, Gail. (1995). *Literature study circles in a multicultural classroom*. York, ME: Stenhouse.

Schlick Noe, Katherine L. & Johnson, Nancy J. (1999). *Getting started with literature circles*. Norwood, MA: Christopher-Gordon.

Smith, Michael W., & Wilhelm, Jeffrey D. (2002). *"Reading don't fix no Chevys": Literacy in the lives of young men*. Portsmouth, NH: Heinemann.

Tovani, Cris. (2000). *I read it, but I don't get it: Comprehension strategies for adolescent readers*. York, ME: Stenhouse.

Trelease, Jim. (1993). *Read all about it!: Great read-aloud stories, poems, and newspaper pieces for preteens and teens*. New York: Penguin.

Wilhelm, Jeffrey. D. (1997). *You gotta BE the book: Teaching engaged and reflective reading with adolescents.* New York: Teachers College Press.

Young Adult Books

Abelove, Joan. (1998). *Go and Come Back.* New York: Dorling Kindersley.

Abelove, Joan. (1999). *Saying It Out Loud.* New York: Dorling Kindersley.

Adoff, Arnold. (1986). *Sports Pages.* New York: HarperCollins.

Adoff, Arnold. (1995). *Street Music: City Poems.* New York: HarperCollins.

Anderson, Laurie Halse. (2000). *Fever 1793.* New York: Simon & Schuster.

Anderson, Rachel. (1993). *The Bus People.* New York: Holt.

Appelt, Kathi. (2000). *Kissing Tennessee and Other Stories From the Stardust Dance.* San Diego: Harcourt Brace.

Asaacs, Anne. (2000). *Torn Thread.* New York: Scholastic.

Avi. (1991). *Nothing But the Truth.* New York: Orchard.

Avi. (1994). *The Barn.* New York: Orchard.

Avi. (1999). *Second Sight: Stories for the New Millennium.* New York: Philomel.

Barre, Shelly. (1993). *Chive.* New York: Simon & Schuster.

Bat-Ami, Miriam. (1999). *Two Suns in the Sky.* New York: Front Street Press.

Bauer, Joan. (1998). *Rules of the Road.* New York: Putnam & Grosset.

Bauer, Joan. (2000). *Hope Was Here.* New York: Putnam.

Bauer, Joan. (2002). *Stand Tall.* New York: Putnam.

Beatty, Patricia. (1981). *Lupita Mañana.* New York: Morrow.

Bechard, Margaret. (2002). *Hanging on to Max*. Brookfield, CT: Millbroook Press.

Berg, Elizabeth. (1993). *Durable Goods*. New York: Avon.

Blackwood, Gary. (1998). *The Shakespeare Stealer*. New York: Dutton.

Blackwood, Gary. (2000). *Shakespeare's Scribe*. New York: Dutton.

Bloor, Edward. (1997). *Tangerine*. San Diego: Harcourt Brace.

Booth, Teena. (2002). *Falling From Fire*. New York: Random House.

Bowler, Tim. (1994). *Midget*. New York: McElderry.

Brooks, Martha. (2000). *Being With Henry*. New York: Dorling Kindersley.

Brownridge, William Roy. (1997). *The Final Game*. New York: Orca Books.

Bruchac, Joseph. (1998). *Heart of a Chief*. New York: Dial.

Buchanan, Lisa Dawna. (1992). *The Falcon's Wing*. New York: Orchard.

Burgess, Melvin. (1992). *Burning Issy*. New York: Simon & Schuster.

Byars, Betsy. (1977). *The Pinballs*. New York: Harper.

Cappo, Nan Willard. (2002). *Cheating Lessons*. New York: Atheneum.

Cart, Michael. (Ed.). (1999). *Tomorrowland: Stories About the Future*. New York: Scholastic.

Carvell, Marlene. (2002). *Who Will Tell My Brother?* New York: Hyperion.

Clements, Andrew. (1999). *The Landry News*. New York: Simon & Schuster.

Clements, Andrew. (2000). *The Janitor's Boy*. New York: Simon & Schuster.

Clements, Andrew. (2002). *Things Not Seen*. New York: Philomel.

Clements, Andrew. (2002). *A Week in the Woods*. New York: Simon & Schuster.

Coleman, Evelyn. (2001). *Born in Sin*. New York: Atheneum.

Coman, Carolyn. (1995). *What Jamie Saw*. Arden, NC: Front Street.

Conly, Jane Leslie. (1993). *Crazy Lady!* New York: HarperCollins.

Cooper, Susan. (1998). *The King of Dragons*. New York: McElderry.

Cooper, Susan. (1999). *King of Shadows*. New York: McElderry.

Cormier, Robert. (1974). *The Chocolate War*. New York: Laurel-Leaf Books.

Couloumbis, Audrey. (1999). *Getting Near to Baby*. New York: G. P. Putnam.

Couloumbis, Audrey. (1999). *Say Yes*. New York: G. P. Putnam.

Coville, Bruce. (Ed.). (1998). *A Glory of Unicorns*. New York: Scholastic.

Coville, Bruce. (1999). *Odder Than Ever*. New York: Harcourt Brace.

Coville, Bruce. (Ed.). (2001). *Half-Human*. New York: Scholastic.

Creech, Sharon. (1994). *Walk Two Moons*. New York: HarperCollins.

Creech, Sharon. (1997). *Chasing Redbird*. New York: HarperCollins.

Creech, Sharon. (2000). *The Wanderer*. New York: HarperCollins.

Creech, Sharon. (2001). *Love That Dog*. New York: HarperCollins.

Creech, Sharon. (2002). *Ruby Holler*. New York: HarperCollins.

Crutcher, Chris. (1991). *Athletic Shorts.* New York: Greenwillow.

Crutcher, Chris. (1993). *Staying Fat for Sarah Byrnes.* New York: Greenwillow.

Crutcher, Chris. (1995). *Ironman.* New York: Greenwillow.

Crutcher, Chris. (2001). *Whale Talk.* New York: Greenwillow.

Cummings, Priscilla. (2001). *A Face First.* New York: Dutton.

Curtis, Christopher Paul. (1995). *The Watsons Go to Birmingham, 1963.* New York: Delacorte.

Curtis, Christopher Paul. (1999). *Bud, Not Buddy.* New York: Delacorte.

Cushman, Karen, (1994). *Catherine, Called Birdy.* New York: Clarion.

Cushman, Karen. (1995). *The Midwife's Apprentice.* New York: Clarion.

Cushman, Karen. (2000). *Matilda Bone.* New York: Clarion.

Dahl, Roald. (1984). *Boy.* New York: Penguin.

Deans, Sis. (2001). *Racing the Past.* New York: Holt.

Dessen, Sarah. (1999). *Keeping the Moon.* New York: Viking.

Deuker, Carl. (1993). *Heart of a Champion.* New York: Joy Street Books.

Dickinson, Peter. (1997). *The Lion Tamer's Daughter and Other Stories.* New York: Delacorte.

Dowell, Frances O'Roark. (2000). *Dovey Coe.* New York: Atheneum.

Duffy, James. (1993). *Radical Red.* New York: Scribner.

Dyer, Daniel. (1997). *Jack London: A Biography.* New York: Scholastic.

Ehrlich, Amy. (Ed.). (1996). *When I Was Your Age: Original Stories About Growing Up.* Cambridge, MA: Candlewick Press.

Ellis, Deborah. (2000). *The Breadwinner*. Toronto, Ontario: Groundwood Books.

Farmer, Nancy. (1994). *The Ear, the Eye, and the Arm*. New York: Orchard.

Farmer, Nancy. (2002). *The House of the Scorpion*. New York: Atheneum.

Feelings, Tom. (Ed.). (1993). *Soul Looks Back in Wonder*. New York: Dial.

Fenner, Carole. (1991). *Randall's Wall*. New York: Macmillan.

Flake, Sharon. (1998). *The Skin I'm In*. New York: Hyperion.

Fleischman, Paul. (1992). *Saturnalia*. New York: HarperCollins.

Fleischman, Paul. (1993). *Bull Run*. New York: HarperCollins.

Fleischman, Paul. (1997). *Seedfolks*. New York: HarperCollins.

Fleischman, Paul. (1998). *Whirligig*. New York: Holt.

Fleischman, Paul. (1999). *Mind's Eye*. New York: Holt.

Fleischman, Paul. (2001). *Seek*. New York: Cricket Books.

Fletcher, Ralph. (1994). *I Am Wings: Poems About Love*. New York: Atheneum.

Fletcher, Ralph. (1996). *Buried Alive: The Elements of Love*. New York: Atheneum.

Fletcher, Ralph. (1997). *Ordinary Things: Poems From a Walk in Early Spring*. New York: Atheneum.

Fletcher, Ralph. (1998). *Flying Solo*. New York: Clarion.

Fogelin, Adrian. (2001). *Anna Casey's Place in the World*. Atlanta, GA: Peachtree.

Fox, Paula. (1997). *Radiance Descending*. New York: Dorling Kindersley.

Fritz, Jean. (1982). *Homesick: My Own Story*. New York: Putnam.

Fuqua, Jonathon Scott. (2002). *Darby*. Cambridge, MA: Candlewick.

Gallo, Donald. (2001). *On the Fringe*. New York: Dial.

Gantos, Jack. (1998). *Joey Pigza Swallowed the Key*. New York: Farrar, Straus & Giroux.

Gantos, Jack. (2000). *Joey Pigza Loses Control*. New York: Farrar, Straus & Giroux.

Garrigue, Sheila. (1985). *The Eternal Spring of Mr. Ito*. New York: Macmillan.

Giff, Patricia Reilly. (1997). *Lily's Crossing*. New York: Delacorte.

Giff, Patricia Reilly. (2001). *All the Way Home*. New York: Delacorte.

Giff, Patricia Reilly. (2002). *Pictures of Hollis Woods*. New York: Random House.

Giles, Gail. (2002). *Shattering Glass*. Brookfield, CT: Millbrook Press.

Gilmore, Kate. (1999). *The Exchange Student*. Boston: Houghton Mifflin.

Grimes, Nikki. (Ed.). (1996). *Shimmy, Shimmy, Shimmy Like My Sister Kate: Looking at Harlem Through Renaissance Poems*. New York: Holt.

Grimes, Nikki. (2002). *Bronx Masquerade*. New York: Dial.

Haddix, Margaret Peterson. (1995). *Running Out of Time*. New York: Simon & Schuster.

Haddix, Margaret Peterson. (1996). *Don't You Dare Read This, Mrs. Dunphrey*. New York: Simon & Schuster.

Haddix, Margaret Peterson. (1998). *Among the Hidden*. New York: Simon & Schuster.

Haddix, Margaret Peterson. (2000). *Turnabout*. New York: Simon & Schuster.

Haddix, Margaret Peterson. (2001). *Among the Imposters*. New York: Simon & Schuster.

Haddix, Margaret Peterson. (2001). *Takeoffs and Landings*. New York: Simon & Schuster.

Haddix, Margaret Peterson. (2002). *Among the Betrayed*. New York: Simon & Schuster.

Hamilton, Virginia. (1990). *Cousins*. New York: Scholastic.

Hamilton, Virginia. (1993). *Plain City*. New York: Scholastic.

Hermes, Patricia. (1991). *Mama, Let's Dance*. New York: Little, Brown.

Hesse, Karen. (1994). *Phoenix Rising*. New York: Holt.

Hesse, Karen. (1997). *Out of the Dust*. New York: Scholastic.

Hesse, Karen. (1998). *Just Juice*. New York: Scholastic.

Hesse, Karen. (2000). *Stowaway*. New York: McElderry.

Hesse, Karen. (2001). *Witness*. New York: Scholastic.

Hinton, S. E. (1967). *The Outsiders*. New York: Viking.

Hirschfelder, Arlene, & Singer, Beverly. (Eds.). (1992). *Rising Voices: Writings of Young Native Americans*. New York: Scribner.

Hobbs, Will. (1991). *Downriver*. New York: Atheneum.

Hobbs, Will. (1996). *Far North*. New York: Morrow.

Hobbs, Will. (1999). *Jason's Gold*. New York: Morrow.

Hobbs, Will. (1999). *The Maze*. New York: Morrow.

Hobbs, Will. (2000). *Down the Yukon*. New York: Morrow.

Holm, Jennifer. (1999). *Our Only May Amelia*. New York: HarperCollins.

Holm, Jennifer. (2001). *Boston Jane: An Adventure*. New York: HarperCollins.

Holt, Kimberly Willis. (1998). *My Louisiana Sky*. New York: Holt.

Holt, Kimberly Willis. (1999). *When Zachary Beaver Came to Town*. New York: Holt.

Holtwijz, Ineke. (1998). *Asphalt Angels*. New York: Front Street Press.

Hopkins, Lee Bennett. (Ed.). (1993). *Extra Innings: Baseball Poems*. New York: Harcourt Brace.

Hopkins, Lee Bennett. (1995). *Been to Yesterday: Poems of a Life*. New York: Boyds Mill Press.

Horvath, Polly. (2001). *Everything on a Waffle*. New York: Farrar, Straus & Giroux.

Howe, James. (Ed.). (2001). *The Color of Absence: 12 Stories About Loss and Hope*. New York: Atheneum.

Howe, James. (2001). *The Misfits*. New York: Atheneum.

Hughes, Dean. (1989). *Family Pose*. New York: Atheneum.

Hughes, Langston. (1996). *The Dream Keeper and Other Poems*. New York: Knopf.

Hurwitz, Johanna. (1995). *Birthday Surprises: Ten Great Stories to Unwrap*. New York: Morrow.

Janeczko, Paul. (Ed.). (1990). *The Place My Words Are Looking For*. New York: Macmillan.

Janeczko, Paul. (Ed.). (2002). *Seeing the Blue Between: Advice and Inspiration for Young Poets*. Cambridge, MA: Candlewick.

Jiang, Ji Li. (1997). *Red Scarf Girl: A Memoir of the Cultural Revolution*. New York: HarperCollins.

Jiménez, Francisco. (1999). *The Circuit*. New York: Houghton Mifflin.

Jiménez, Francisco. (2001). *Breaking Through*. New York: Houghton Mifflin.

Johnson, Angela. (1993). *Toning the Sweep*. New York: Orchard.

Johnson, Angela. (1998). *Heaven*. New York: Simon & Schuster.

Jones, Charlotte Foltz. (1999). *Yukon Gold: The Story of the Klondike Gold Rush*. New York: Holiday House.

Kehret, Peg. (1991). *Cages*. New York: Dutton.

Koertge, Ron. (2001). *The Brimstone Journals*. New York: Candlewick.

Koller, Jackie French. (1995). *A Place to Call Home*. New York: Atheneum.

Konigsburg, E. L. (1996). *The View From Saturday*. New York: Atheneum.

Konigsburg, E. L. (2000). *Silent to the Bone*. New York: Atheneum.

Korman, Gordon. (2000). *No More Dead Dogs*. New York: Hyperion.

Koss, Amy Goldman. (2000). *The Girls*. New York: Dial.

Krisher, Trudy. (1994). *Spite Fences*. New York: Deleacote.

Krisher, Trudy. (1997). *Kinship*. New York: Delacorte.

Kurtz, Jane. (1998). *The Storyteller's Beads*. San Diego: Harcourt Brace.

LaFaye, A. (1998). *The Year of the Sawdust Man*. New York: Simon & Schuster.

LaFaye, A. (1999). *Nissa's Place*. New York: Simon & Schuster.

LaFaye, A. (1999). *Strawberry Hill*. New York: Simon & Schuster.

Lasky, Kathryn. (1994). *Memoirs of a Bookbat*. San Diego: Harcourt Brace.

Lasky, Kathryn. (1999). *Elizabeth I: Red Rose of the House of Tudor, England 1544*. New York: Scholastic.

Lasky, Kathryn. (1999). *Star Split*. New York: Hyperion.

Lawrence, Iain. (1999). *The Wreckers*. New York: Delacorte.

Lawrence, Iain. (2000). *Ghost Boy*. New York: Delacorte.

L'Engle, Madeleine. (1962). *A Wrinkle in Time*. New York: Farrar, Straus & Giroux.

Levine, Gail Carson. (1999). *Dave at Night*. New York: HarperCollins.

Levine, Garl Carson. (2000). *The Wish*. New York: HarperCollins.

Levitin, Sonia. (1999). *The Cure*. San Diego: Harcourt Brace.

London, Jack. (1903). *The Call of the Wild*. New York: Grosset.

Lourie, Peter. (2000). *Yukon River: An Adventure to the Gold Fields of the Klondike.* Honesdale, PA: Boyds Mills Press.

Lowry, Lois. (1986). *Autumn Street*. New York: Yearling.

Lowry, Lois. (1993). *The Giver*. New York: Houghton Mifflin.

Lowry, Lois. (2000). *Gathering Blue*. New York: Houghton Mifflin.

Lutzeier, Elizabeth. (1991). *The Wall*. New York: Holiday House.

Lynch, Chris. (1995). *Slot Machine*. New York: HarperCollins.

MacLachlan, Patricia (1991). *Journey*. New York: Dell.

Magorian, Michelle. (1981). *Goodnight, Mr. Tom*. New York: HarperCollins.

Marsden, John. (1991). *Letters From Inside*. Boston, MA: Houghton Mifflin.

Marsden, John. (1995). *Tomorrow When the War Began*. Boston, MA: Houghton Mifflin.

Martin, Ann M. (2001). *Belle Teal*. New York: Scholastic.

Martin, Nora. (1997). *The Eagle's Shadow*. New York: Scholastic.

Martinez, Victor. (1996). *Parrot in the Oven: Mi Vida*. New York: HarperCollins.

Mazer, Harry. (1997). *Twelve Shots: Outstanding Short Stories About Guns*. New York: Delacorte.

McDonald, Janet. (2001). *Spellbound*. New York: Farrar, Straus & Giroux.

McKinley, Robin. (1994). *A Knot in the Grain and Other Stories*. New York: Greenwillow.

McKinley, Robin & Dickinson, Peter. (2002). *Water: Tales of Elemental Spirits*. New York: Putnam.

McLaren, Clemence. (2000). *Waiting for Odysseus*. New York: Atheneum.

Meyer, Carolyn. (1995). *Drummers of Jericho*. New York: Gulliver Books.

Meyer, Carolyn. (1999). *Mary, Bloody Mary*. San Diego: Harcourt Brace.

Meyer, Carolyn. (2001). *Beware, Princess Elizabeth*. San Diego: Harcourt Brace.

Mikaelsen, Ben. (1998). *Petey*. New York: Hyperion.

Mills, Claudia. (1998). *Standing Up to Mr. O*. New York: Farrar, Straus & Giroux.

Mori, Kyoko. (1993). *Shizuko's Daughter*. New York: Holt.

Mosher, Richard. (2001). *Zazoo*. New York: Clarion.

Myers, Walter Dean. (1983). *Hoops*. New York: Delacorte.

Myers, Walter Dean. (1988). *Scorpions*. New York: HarperCollins.

Myers, Walter Dean. (1999). *Monster*. New York: HarperCollins.

Myers, Walter Dean. (2000). *145th Street: Short Stories*. New York: Delacorte.

Napoli, Donna Jo. (1997). *Stones in Water*. New York: Dutton.

Naylor, Phyllis Reynolds. (1999). *Walker's Crossing*. New York: Atheneum.

Nelson, Theresa. (1994). *Earthshine*. New York: Orchard.

Nelson, Theresa. (1998). *The Empress of Elsewhere*. New York: Dorling Kindersley.

Nixon, Joan Lowry. (1987). *A Family Apart*. New York: Bantam.

Nolan, Han. (1999). *A Face in Every Window*. New York: Penguin.

Nye, Naomi Shihab. (1997). *Habibi*. New York: Simon & Schuster.

Nye, Naomi Shihab. (Ed.). (1998). *The Flag of Childhood: Poems From the Middle East*. New York: Simon & Schuster.

Nye, Naomi Shihab. (2002). *19 Varieties of Gazelle: Poems of the Middle East*. New York: Greenwillow.

Nye, Naomi Shihab & Janeczko, Paul. (Eds.). (1996). *I Feel a Little Jumpy Around You*. New York: Simon & Schuster.

O'Brien, Robert C. (1974). *Z for Zachariah*. New York: Macmillan.

O'Connor, Barbara. (2001). *Moonpie and Ivy*. New York: Farrar, Straus & Giroux.

Olson, Gretchen. (1998). *Joyride*. Honesdale, PA: Boyds Mills Press.

Orr, Wendy. (1996). *Peeling the Onion*. New York: Holiday House.

Oughton, Jerrie. (1995). *Music From a Place Called Half Moon*. New York: Doubleday.

Pace, Sue. (1993). *The Oasis*. New York: Delacorte.

Park, Barbara. (1995). *Mick Harte Was Here*. New York: Knopf.

Park, Barbara. (2000). *The Graduation of Jake Moon*. New York: Atheneum.

Park, Linda Sue. (2002). *When My Name Was Keoko*. New York: Clarion.

Paterson, Katherine. (1978). *The Great Gilly Hopkins*. New York: Crowell.

Paterson, Katherine. (1991). *Lyddie*. New York: Lodestar.

Paterson, Katherine. (1994). *Flip-Flop Girl*. New York: Lodestar.

Paterson, Katherine. (1996). *Jip: His Story*. New York: Lodestar.

Paulsen, Gary. (1993). *Harris and Me*. San Diego: Harcourt Brace.

Paulsen, Gary. (1993). *Nightjohn*. New York: Delacorte.

Paulsen, Gary. (1997). *Sarny: A Life Remembered*. New York: Delacorte.

Paulsen, Gary. (1998). *My Life in Dog Years*. New York: Delacorte.

Paulsen, Gary. (1999). *Alida's Song*. New York: Delacorte.

Paulsen, Gary. (2001). *Guts*. New York: Delacorte.

Peck, Richard. (1995). *The Last Safe Place on Earth*. New York: Delacorte.

Peck, Richard. (1998). *A Long Way From Chicago*. New York: Dial.

Peck, Richard. (2000). *A Year Down Yonder*. New York: Dial.

Perkins, Lynne Rae. (1999). *All Alone in the Universe*. New York: Greenwillow.

Philbrick, W. Rodman. (1993). *Freak the Mighty*. New York: Scholastic.

Philbrick, W. Rodman. (1998). *Max the Mighty*. New York: Scholastic.

Philbrick, W. Rodman. (2000). *The Last Book in the Universe*. New York: Scholastic.

Platt, Randall Beth. (2000). *The Likes of Me*. New York: Delacorte.

Powell, Randy. (1999). *Tribute to Another Dead Rock Star*. New York: Farrar, Straus & Giroux.

Pullman, Philip. (1995). *The Golden Compass*. New York: Knopf.

Pullman, Philip. (1997). *The Subtle Knife*. New York: Knopf.

Pullman, Philip. (2000). *The Amber Spyglass*. New York: Knopf.

Quarles, Heather. (1998). *A Door Near Here*. New York: Delacorte.

Reeder, Carolyn. (1998). *Foster's War*. New York: Scholastic.

Rinaldi, Ann. (2002). *Numbering All the Bones.* New York: Hyperion.

Robinet, Harriet Gillem. (2000). *Walking to the Bus-Rider Blues.* New York: Atheneum.

Robinson, Margaret. (1990). *A Woman of Her Tribe.* New York: Fawcett.

Rochman, Hazel. (Ed.). (1990). *Somehow Tenderness Survives: Stories of Southern Africa.* New York: Harper.

Rodowsky, Colby. (1996). *Hannah in Between.* New York: Farrar, Straus & Giroux.

Rosen, Michael. (1992). *Home.* New York: HarperCollins.

Ryan, Pam Muñoz. (2000). *Esperanza Rising.* New York: Scholastic.

Rylant, Cynthia. (1992). *Missing May.* New York: Orchard.

Sachar, Louis. (1998). *Holes.* New York: Farrar, Straus & Giroux.

Sachs, Marilyn. (1982). *Call Me Ruth.* New York: Doubleday.

Salisbury, Graham. (1994). *Under the Blood Red Sun.* New York: Delacorte.

Shetterly, Will. (1997). *Dogland.* New York: Tom Doherty.

Singer, Marilyn. (Ed.). (1998). *Stay True: Short Stories for Strong Girls.* New York: Scholastic.

Slepian, Jan. (1990). *Risk 'n Roses.* New York: Philomel.

Smith, Roland. (1995). *Thunder Cave.* New York: Hyperion.

Smith, Sherri. (2002). *Lucy the Giant.* New York: Delacorte.

Sones, Sonya. (2001). *What My Mother Doesn't Know.* New York: Simon & Schuster.

Soto, Gary. (1990). *Baseball in April and Other Stories.* San Diego: Harcourt Brace.

Soto, Gary. (1992). *Neighborhood Odes.* San Diego: Harcourt.

Spinelli, Jerry. (1990). *Maniac Magee.* New York: Little, Brown.

Spinelli, Jerry. (1996). *Crash*. New York: Knopf.

Spinelli, Jerry. (1997). *Wringer*. New York: HarperCollins.

Spinelli, Jerry. (1998). *Knots in My Yo-Yo String*. New York: Knopf.

Spinelli, Jerry. (2000). *Stargirl*. New York: Knopf.

Spinelli, Jerry. (2002). *Loser*. New York: HarperCollins.

Staples, Suzanne Fisher. (1989). *Shabanu: Daughter of the Wind*. New York: Knopf.

Staples, Suzanne Fisher. (1998). *Dangerous Skies*. New York: Harper Trophy.

Strasser, Todd. (2000). *Give a Boy a Gun*. New York: Simon & Schuster.

Taylor, Mildred. (1975). *Song of the Trees*. New York: Dial.

Taylor, Mildred. (1976). *Roll of Thunder, Hear My Cry*. New York: Viking.

Taylor, Mildred. (1981). *Let the Circle Be Unbroken*. New York: Dial.

Taylor, Mildred. (1998). *The Gold Cadillac*. New York: Puffin.

Taylor, Mildred. (2001). *The Land*. New York: Penguin Putnam.

Taylor, Theodore. (1969). *The Cay*. New York: Avon.

Thesman, Jean. (1991). *The Rain Catchers*. New York: Houghton.

Thesman, Jean. (1996). *When the Road Ends*. New York: Houghton.

Thomson, Sarah L. (2001) *The Dragon's Son*. New York: Orchard.

Trueman, Terry. (2000). *Stuck in Neutral*. New York: HarperCollins.

Turner, Ann. (2000). *Learning to Swim: A Memoir*. New York: Scholastic.

Uchida, Yoshiko. (1971). *Journey to Topaz*. New York: Scribner.

Uchida, Yoshiko. (1978). *Journey Home*. New York: Atheneum.

Uchida, Yoshiko. (1992). *The Invisible Thread*. New York: Messner.

Van Draanen, Wendelin. (2001). *Flipped*. New York: Knopf.

Voigt, Cynthia. (1981). *Homecoming*. New York: Atheneum.

Voigt, Cynthia. (1982). *Dicey's Song*. Random House.

Watkins, Yoko Kawashima. (1986). *So Far From the Bamboo Grove*. New York: Lothrop, Lee & Shepard.

Weiss, M. Jerry and Weiss, Helen. (Eds.). (1997). *From One Experience to Another: Award-winning Authors Sharing Real-life Experiences Through Fiction*. New York: Tom Doherty.

Whelan, Gloria. (2001). *Angel on the Square*. New York: HarperCollins.

White, Ruth. (1996). *Belle Prater's Boy*. New York: Farrar, Straus & Giroux.

White, Ruth. (2000). *Memories of Summer*. New York: Farrar, Straus & Giroux.

Wiles, Deborah. (2001). *Love, Ruby Lavender*. San Diego: Harcourt.

Wilhelm, Doug. (2001). *Raising the Shade*. New York: Farrar, Straus & Giroux.

Willard, Nancy. (Ed.). (1998). *Step Lightly: Poems for the Journey*. San Diego: Harcourt Brace.

Williams, Carol Lynch. (1998). *The True Colors of Caitlynne Jackson*. New York: Dell.

Wolff, Virginia Euwer. (1988). *Probably Still Nick Swanson*. New York: Holt.

Wolff, Virginia Euwer. (1993). *Make Lemonade*. New York: Holt.

Wolff, Virginia Euwer. (1998). *Bat 6*. New York: Scholastic.

Wolff, Virginia Euwer. (2001). *True Believer*. New York: Atheneum.

Wong, Janet. (1996). *A Suitcase of Seaweed and Other Poems*. New York: McElderry.

Wong, Janet. (1999). *Behind the Wheel: Poems About Driving*. New York: McElderry.

Woodson, Jacqueline. (2000). *Miracle's Boys*. New York: Scholastic.

Wynne-Jones, Tim. (1996). *The Maestro*. New York: Orchard.

Yee, Paul. (1997). *Breakaway*. New York: Douglas & McIntyre.

Yep, Laurence. (1991). *The Star Fisher*. New York: Scholastic.

Young, Ronder Thomas. (1997). *Moving Mama to Town*. New York: Orchard.

Index

A

ALAN Review, The (NCTE), 32
Allen, Janet, 10, 51
Alvermann, Donna E., 10
Ambrosini, Michelle, 10
American Library Association: Young
    Adult Library Services Association
    (YALSA), 32
Atwell, Nancie, 10
Avi, 78

B

Barbieri, Maureen, 31
Barre, Shelley, 36
Bauer, Joan, 36
Beatty, Patricia, 21
Benson, Laura, 28, 62
Beware, Princess Elizabeth (Meyer,
    2001), 1, 30
Blackwood, Gary, 1, 22, 27
Bloor, Edward, 36, 66, 78
Book Links (American Library
    Association), 31, 32
Book Club for Middle School (Raphael,
    Kehus, & Damphousse, 2001), 10
Book talk, 7, 30, 31
Bookmark, ix, x, 15, 44
Boy (Dahl, 1984), 20
Breadwinner, The (Ellis, 2000), 29
Brozo, William G., 10
Burke, Carolyn, 72

C

Call of the Wild (London, 1903), 73
Chevalier, Tracy, 43
Children's Literature Web Guide, 32
Chive (Barre, 1993), 36
Chocolate War, The (Cormier, 1974),
    27
Choosing books
  Criteria, 26
    Background knowledge, 27–28
    Book appeal, 27
    Curricular match, 30
    Depth, engagement, and
        appropriate content, 26–27
    Diversity, 28–29
    Gender balance, 29
    Genre variety, 30
    Text difficulty, 28
  Keeping up with new books, ix, 30–
    32
  Obtaining multiple copies, 33
    "Wish list", 34
    Bonus points, 33
    Book exchange, 34
  Online resources, 31
  Read aloud, 36
  Selecting books for different grades,
    34–35
Circuit, The (Jiménez, 1999), 21
Classroom Based Assessment (Hill,
    Ruptic, & Norwick, 1998), 55
Combs, Martha, 3, 10

How to Use
the CD-ROM

The CD-ROM accompanying this book contains a Database of Young Adult Books. The Database of Young Adult Books was created with Filemaker® and is distributed in a royalty-free runtime version. No additional software is required. The Database of Young Adult Books requires approximately 7MB of disk space and must be installed on your hard drive to use.

Windows 95/98/XP/NT
Installation and System Requirements

To install the program, run SETUP.EXE on the CD-ROM. Double-click "My Computer", double-click the CD-ROM icon for "Literature Circles in Middle School," then double-click "SETUP.EXE" and follow the directions on the screen.

To run the program, double-click the appropriate icon on the desktop (Database of Young Adult Books) or start the program from the Windows Start Menu (Start > Programs > Database of Young Adult Books).

Minimum PC System Requirements:

- Intel Compatible 486/33MHz PC (recommended 133MHz Pentium)
- At least 16 MB of RAM (recommended 32 MB)
- Hard disk with at least 20 MB of free space
- CD-ROM drive
- 600 x 800 pixel minimum video screen area

- Windows 95 with Internet Explorer 4.0 or later, Windows 98, Windows XP, or Windows NT 4.0 (with Service Pack 3 or later)

To remove the programs from your computer, open Windows Control Panel and then select Add/Remove Programs. Highlight "Database of Young Adult Books" and select "Add/Remove".

Mac OS Installation and System Requirements

To install the Database of Young Adult Books, drag the folder "Database of Young Adult Books" from the CD-ROM to your hard drive.

To open the Database of Young Adult Books, open the "Database of Young Adult Books" folder on your hard disk and double-click the DATABASE file icon.

Minimum Mac System Requirements:

- Power Macintosh or Mac OS computer with a PPC 601 processor or higher
- At least 16 MB of RAM (recommended 32 MB)
- Hard disk with at least 24 MB of free space (54 MB if the CD-ROM Resources are installed)
- CD-ROM drive
- 600 x 800 pixel minimum video screen area
- System 8.1 or later

About the Authors

Bonnie Campbell Hill taught elementary school in Boulder, Colorado and Seattle, Washington. She received her doctorate in Reading/Language Arts from the University of Washington. She is currently a national and international consultant in the area of literacy, children's literature, and assessment. She is the author/co-author of the following books: *Developmental Continuums* (Hill, 2001), *The Literature Circles Resource Guide* (Hill, Schlick Noe, & Johnson, 2000), *Classroom Based Assessment* (Hill, Ruptic, & Norwick, 1998), *Literature Circles and Response* (Edited by Hill, Johnson & Schlick Noe, 1995), and *Practical Aspects of Authentic Assessment: Putting the Pieces Together* (Hill & Ruptic, 1994).

Katherine L. Schlick Noe is Professor of Education and Director of Literacy at Seattle University. A former high school teacher, she received her Ph.D. in Reading/Language Arts from the University of Washington. Katherine is co-editor of *Literature Circles and Response* with Bonnie Campbell Hill and Nancy J. Johnson; co-author of *Getting Started with Literature Circles* with Nancy J. Johnson; and co-author of *Literature Circles Resource Guide* with Bonnie Campbell Hill and Nancy J. Johnson, all published by Christopher-Gordon.

Janine A. King is a middle school language arts teacher at Brighton School in Lynnwood, Washington. Prior to teaching middle school for nine years, she taught fourth grade. Janine received her M.Ed. in Curriculum and Instruction with a Specialization in Reading from Seattle University. She has published in *Northwest Reading Journal* and contributes book reviews to the children's book column in *The Reading Teacher*.